G000146573

Dear Gordon.

Happy Birthday.

Best wishes from all of us !

COMFORT
FOOD

COMFORT FOOD

JUST LIKE MOTHER USED TO MAKE:
150 HEART-WARMING DISHES SHOWN
IN OVER 200 EVOCATIVE PHOTOGRAPHS

Bridget Jones

LORENZ BOOKS

This edition is published by Lorenz Books,
an imprint of Anness Publishing Ltd,
Blaby Road, Wigston, Leicestershire LE18 4SE

info@anness.com; www.lorenzbooks.com;
www.annesspublishing.com

If you like the images in this book and would like
to investigate using them for publishing, promotions
or advertising, please visit our website
www.practicalpictures.com for more information.

Publisher: Joanna Lorenz
Editorial director: Helen Sudell
Project editor: Emma Clegg
Designer: Nigel Partridge
Production controller: Christine Ni

Main image on front cover: Bakewell Tart (see page 190)

© Anness Publishing Ltd 2011

All rights reserved. No part of this publication may be
reproduced, stored in a retrieval system, or transmitted
in any way or by any means, electronic, mechanical,
photocopying, recording or otherwise, without the prior
written permission of the copyright holder.

A CIP catalogue record for this book is available from
the British Library.

PUBLISHER'S NOTE
Although the advice and information in this book
are believed to be accurate and true at the time of
going to press, neither the authors nor the publisher
can accept any legal responsibility or liability for any
errors or omissions that may have been made nor
for any inaccuracies nor for any loss, harm or injury
that comes about from following instructions or
advice in this book.

ETHICAL TRADING POLICY
At Anness Publishing we believe that business
should be conducted in an ethical and ecologically
sustainable way, with respect for the environment
and a proper regard to the replacement of the natural
resources we employ.

As a publisher, we use a lot of wood pulp in
high-quality paper for printing, and that wood
commonly comes from spruce trees. We are therefore
currently growing more than 750,000 trees in three
Scottish forest plantations: Berrymoss (130 hectares/
320 acres), West Touxhill (125 hectares/305 acres) and
Deveron Forest (75 hectares/185 acres). The forests we
manage contain more than 3.5 times the number of
trees employed each year in making paper for the
books we manufacture.

Because of this ongoing ecological investment
programme, you, as our customer, can have the
pleasure and reassurance of knowing that a tree is
being cultivated on your behalf to naturally replace the
materials used to make the book you are holding.

Our forestry programme is run in accordance with the
UK Woodland Assurance Scheme (UKWAS) and will be
certified by the internationally recognized Forest
Stewardship Council (FSC). The FSC is a non-government
organization dedicated to promoting responsible
management of the world's forests. Certification ensures
forests are managed in an environmentally sustainable
and socially responsible way. For further information
about this scheme, go to www.annesspublishing.com/trees

NOTES
For all recipes, quantities are given in both
metric and imperial measures and, where
appropriate, measures are also given in standard
cups and spoons. Follow one set, but not a
mixture, because they are not interchangeable.

Standard spoon and cup measures are level.
1 tsp = 5ml, 1 tbsp = 15ml, 1 cup = 250ml/8fl oz

Australian standard tablespoons are 20ml.
Australian readers should use 3 tsp in place of
1 tbsp for measuring small quantities

American pints are 16fl oz/2 cups. American
readers should use 20fl oz/2.5 cups in place of
1 pint when measuring liquids.

Electric oven temperatures in this book are for
conventional ovens. When using a fan oven, the
temperature will probably need to be reduced by
about 10–20°C/20–40°F. Since ovens vary, you
should check with your manufacturer's
instruction book for guidance.

The nutritional analysis given for each recipe is
calculated per portion (i.e. serving or item),
unless otherwise stated. If the recipe gives a
range, such as Serves 4–6, then the nutritional
analysis will be for the smaller portion size, i.e. 6
servings. The analysis does not include optional
ingredients, such as salt added to taste.

Medium (US large) eggs are used unless
otherwise stated.

Contents

Introduction

Comfort food can be a lazy lie-in with a bacon sandwich and a cup of tea or it may be eating a pizza on a rainy afternoon as you watch an old movie. It's whatever makes you feel good – you've found it if it lifts your spirits, warms you when you're cold or revives you when you're weary.

It is true that everyone has different ideas of what constitutes true comfort food – individual preferences might be creamy, sweet, spicy, or salty. What is universal is that the tastes of these foods appeal directly to our body's feel-good responses. Foods that we enjoy eating often have pleasant associations and are hard to resist. Our favourite dishes might be based on childhood memories of times when we felt safe and secure, enjoyable holidays abroad, or special celebration treats. Eating pleasurable food is deeply satisfying; it relieves us of our hunger and makes us feel content. When our hunger is satisfied after a meal that we have enjoyed, all is well with our world. We have rebalanced our blood-sugar levels to give us energy, and our mood is restored to good humour.

Everybody likes to eat, and while not all of us like to cook, it's true that most of us are capable of rustling up food that makes us feel better. Many favourite comfort foods are simple offerings that can be made easily: hot toast dripping with salty butter and flavourful, fruity jam; a thick slab of moist cake with a mug of strong coffee; a soft cheese and crunchy salad sandwich, topped with tangy pickle; or home-baked cookies dunked in a cup of tea.

With ease of cooking in mind, all of the recipes in this book are no-fuss, everyday dishes, made with ingredients that are readily available. None of them involve complicated cooking methods, though some do take time to cook. What they have in common is an appeal to a basic instinct in all of us. Food nurtures the body and nourishes the soul.

Eating is essential, and we all enjoy good, flavourful food, preferably in the company of good friends or family. The recipes can be eaten alone, or combined with others. Some are suitable for large numbers of people, while others are single servings, but can be multiplied to suit the occasion.

LEFT: *Old-fashioned chicken soup.*

ABOVE: *Cranachan.*

ABOVE: *Egg mayonnaise sandwich.*

ABOVE: *Mixed bean and tomato chilli.*

One or two are best cooked ahead for eating the next day, so that flavours have a chance to mature, and some can be cooked and kept in the refrigerator to provide emergency comfort stocks. To that end, here is a delicious collection of 150 appealing, tried-and-tested recipes from all over the world. They taste divine, will satisfy your appetite, feed your family and make you feel good.

As well as traditional staples such as apple pie, roast dinners and nursery recipes like fish pie, the dishes also include contemporary interpretations of older recipes, bringing the comfort factor up to date. For example a classic bread and butter pudding has here been transformed into a superbly rich, textural delight in hazelnut and pain au chocolat pudding.

Take note that comfort food does not necessarily mean unhealthy eating or slipping into a haze of sugar, cream and chocolate, although a few of these recipes might be kept for special treats. It's really about unhurried menu planning, choosing familiar ingredients, pleasurable shopping trips and effortless food preparation.

Knowing that the food we serve has been made using the freshest ingredients just before it's about to be consumed adds to our nurturing instincts. A home-cooked dish of piping hot food as we arrive home on a cold day is a welcome pleasure; the warmth of the kitchen and the aroma of cooking both add to our emotional response to food. Likewise a warm, milky drink in the evening, before we go to bed, will make us content and sleepy. Some foods are calming and warming, while others are energy-giving, and make us feel alert and ready to face the day. For many of us, the types of food that we like to eat may be a subconscious reaction to their effect once consumed.

One feature of the recipes is the presence of excellent ingredients from around the world. Most people's

ABOVE: *Meatballs in tomato sauce.*

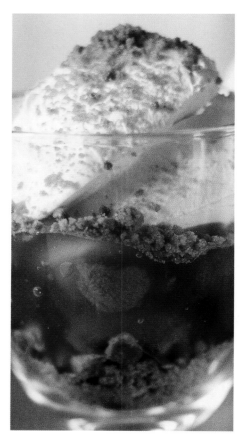

ABOVE: *Rhubarb and ginger trifle.*

ABOVE: *Waffles with blueberry compote.*

palates are quite sophisticated these days, and unusual foodstuffs are increasingly easy to find, so it's not necessary to stay in the nursery to get the "oooh!" factor. Just thinking about the range of pasta and rice, the huge selection of vegetables, herbs and spices, oils, vinegars and breads that are now on offer, makes your head spin. These ingredients bring alive old classics, enhancing flavours and delighting in differing textures.

Whether sourced from European, American, Australian or Thai cuisines, comfort food knows no boundaries. Among many examples we have Sicilian Brioche Breakfast, French Rarebit, Bakewell Tart from the UK,

Leche Frita from Spain, Turkish Baklava, Scandinavian Creamy Egg Nog, Prawn Laksa from southeast Asia, and Shoofly Pie and Southern-fried Chicken from the USA.

No matter what the origins of the recipes, the essence of all comfort food is that it is home-made. This is because the recipes are as enjoyable to plan and prepare as they are to eat. Taking pleasure in the ingredients, equipment, cooking and serving are all part of the comfort. There's something very reassuring about being in your own kitchen, handling utensils you've grown to cherish, such as a well-seasoned pancake pan or a really good wok, or setting out

favourite coffee cups alongside the coffee pot and the freshly-made scones and jam on a tray given you by a friend. Sometimes just the planning, shopping and buying, preparation and serving is extremely comforting, and the eating a wonderful bonus.

Recipes are divided into sections that correspond to meals and snacks at different times of day. Starting with Lazy Breakfasts and Brunches, you might hanker after a Crunchy Breakfast Muffin with your first coffee of the day, or perhaps some Drop Scones with Bacon and Maple Syrup. Sustaining Lunches include a warming recipe for Tomato Soup with Black Olive Ciabatta Toasts or Prawn and Dill Tartlets with buttery shortcrust pastry. Coffee and Teatime Treats is a section simply bursting with sweet treats for between meals, such as the ever-popular American Chocolate Brownie or the smooth, satisfying chewyness of Coconut Cakes.

As a choice for a Satisfying Vegetarian Supper, why not opt for the creamy Alfredo's Fettucine or the flavourful and healthy Italian Stuffed Peppers? For Comforting Fish and Meat Dishes the choice includes Niçoise Noodle Salad with Seared Tuna and Lemon Grass and Coconut Rice with Green Chicken Curry, or for red meat lovers Steak and Mushroom Pudding. Then you can relax with one of a selection of Chill-out Desserts, from Rhubarb and Ginger Trifle to a Summer Pudding with seasonal soft fruits, or alternatively follow the Hot Pudding route and partake of Waffles with Spiced Blueberry Compote or the delicious Baked Bananas with Hazelnut Sauce. The final section is a special one called Sweet Asides that includes self-indulgent sweets and delicious drinks – notable highlights here are Turkish Delight, Espresso-macadamia Fudge, Passionata Milkshake with ripe passion fruit and sweet caramel, or a hot toddy to warm the cockles of your heart on a winter's evening.

All of these examples slide seamlessly into the comfort category. Many of the recipes

featured here are easily transported, allowing you to enjoy a snack or meal wherever you are relaxing, be that the bedroom, living room or kitchen table. If hunger strikes when you're sprawled on the rug playing a board game, or sitting on the sofa immersed in the television, it makes sense to prepare food and drink you can enjoy just where you are. With the exception of some heartier dishes designed for sharing with

family and friends at the table, all the recipes here are intended for easy eating.

Enjoying food and its various aromas, tastes and textures is one of life's great pleasures. The delicious recipes here cover every meal and occasion, from breakfast to midnight snacks. Whether savoury or sweet, chilled or warm, self-indulgent titbits or substantial meals, cooking these dishes will bring sunshine to your day.

RIGHT: *Chocolate brownie milkshake.*

Lazy Breakfasts and Brunches

Perhaps a slice of toast, a banana or cereal is all you have time for first thing in the morning. So weekends and holidays are the times to enjoy extravagant and lazy breakfasts, and these may well stretch into brunch. This chapter is full of soothing, satisfying and utterly self-indulgent ideas for the first meal of the day, from flaky morning pastries to fabulous fry-ups. And remember, none of them should be rushed.

Cranachan

This is based on a traditional Scottish recipe originally made to celebrate the Harvest Festival.
Cool, refreshing and nutritious, this scores high both as a special treat and as a healthy dish.

SERVES 4

75g/3oz crunchy oat cereal
600ml/1 pint/2½ cups Greek
   (US strained plain) yogurt
250g/9oz/1⅓ cups raspberries
heather honey, to serve

VARIATION
You can use almost any berries
for this recipe. Strawberries and
blackberries work very well. If you use
strawberries, remove the stalks and cut
them into quarters beforehand.

1 Preheat the grill (broiler) to high. Spread the oat cereal on a baking sheet and place under the hot grill for 3–4 minutes, stirring regularly. Set aside on a plate to cool.

2 When the cereal has cooled, fold it into the Greek yogurt, then gently fold in 200g/7oz/generous 1 cup of the raspberries, being careful not to crush them.

3 Spoon the yogurt mixture into four serving glasses or dishes, top with the remaining raspberries and serve immediately. Pass around a dish of heather honey to drizzle over the top for extra sweetness and flavour.

Nutritional information per portion: Energy 276kcal/1152kJ; Protein 12.4g; Carbohydrate 17.2g, of which sugars 11.1g; Fat 19.7g, of which saturates 8.7g; Cholesterol 0mg; Calcium 255mg; Fibre 2.5g; Sodium 122mg.

Real porridge with plums

On cold days there is nothing better than a bowl of warm porridge. Whether to add salt or sugar is completely up to you – it is also delightful with cream and honey.

SERVES 4

300ml/¹⁄₂ pint/1¹⁄₄ cups fruity red wine
75g/3oz/scant ¹⁄₂ cup caster (superfine) sugar
1 cinnamon stick
1 star anise
450g/1lb red or purple plums
115g/4oz/1 cup medium oatmeal
salt
single (light) or double (heavy) cream, to serve

1 To poach the plums, pour the wine into a pan and stir in the sugar. Add the cinnamon stick and the star anise. Bring to the boil and boil for about 1 minute.

2 Halve and stone (pit) the plums. Add the plums to the wine syrup and barely simmer for 10 minutes until beginning to soften. Allow to cool.

3 To make the porridge pour 1 litre/1³⁄₄ pints/4 cups water into a pan and bring to the boil.

4 Tip in the oatmeal, stirring to stop lumps from forming. Turn down the heat and simmer for 10–15 minutes, or until the porridge is as thick as you like it. Season with salt to taste.

5 Pour the porridge into deep, warmed bowls and serve the plums alongside, with cold cream in a separate bowl. Take a spoonful of porridge and dip it into the cream. Eat this, then take a spoonful of plums. Savour the contrast – this is not a dish to be hurried.

Nutritional information per portion: Energy 268kcal/1136kJ; Protein 4g; Carbohydrate 44g, of which sugars 25g; Fat 2.5g, of which saturates 0.5g; Cholesterol 0mg; Calcium 31mg; Fibre 3g; Sodium 171mg.

Crunchy breakfast muffins

Toasted oat cereals make a delicious and crunchy addition to these moreish muffins. The raisins add a sweetness to the light texture of this batter. Serve with strong coffee.

MAKES 10 STANDARD MUFFINS

150g/5oz/1¼ cups plain (all-purpose) flour
7.5ml/1½ tsp baking powder
30ml/2 tbsp caster (superfine) sugar
250ml/8fl oz/1 cup full cream (whole) milk
1 egg
50g/2oz/¼ cup butter, melted
200g/7oz toasted oat cereal and raisins, mixed

1 Preheat the oven to 350°F/180°C/Gas 4. Lightly grease the cups of a muffin tin (pan) or line them with paper cases.

2 Sift the flour into a bowl. Add the baking powder, then the sugar and stir in. Make a well in the centre.

3 In a jug (pitcher), using a fork, beat the milk with the egg and the melted butter.

4 Pour the liquid into the well in the flour mixture. Stir lightly until just combined.

5 Stir in the cereal and raisins. Bake for 20–22 minutes until risen and golden. Leave to cool in the tin (pan) for a few minutes, then turn out on to a wire rack to go cold. Serve fresh, or store in an airtight container for up to 3 days.

Nutritional information per portion: Energy 180kcal/759kJ; Protein 4.6g; Carbohydrate 29.8g, of which sugars 10.8g; Fat 5.6g, of which saturates 3.2g; Cholesterol 32mg; Calcium 68mg; Fibre 2.5g; Sodium 210mg.

Berry brioche muffins

A traditional sweet brioche recipe is studded with fresh blueberries, making a luxurious muffin. For a special breakfast treat, enjoy them warm, spread with blueberry or cherry jam.

MAKES 10 LARGE MUFFINS

15g/¹/₂oz fresh yeast

4 medium (US large) eggs

350g/12oz/3 cups plain (all-purpose)
    flour

50g/2oz/¹/₄ cup caster (superfine) sugar

10g/¹/₄oz salt

175g/6oz/³/₄ cup unsalted butter,
    softened

115g/4oz/1 cup blueberries

45ml/3 tbsp full cream (whole) milk, for
    the eggwash

1 small egg yolk, for the eggwash

COOK'S TIP

*Prepare the brioche dough a day ahead
of making the muffins.*

1 Crumble the yeast into a food processor or blender fitted with a dough hook. Add 10ml/2 tsp warm water and combine. Add the eggs, flour, sugar and salt. Beat at low speed for 6–7 minutes. Turn up to a moderate speed and add the butter. Beat for 12–15 minutes until the dough is smooth and shiny. Seal the dough in a plastic bag and chill for 24 hours, or overnight.

2 Grease the cups of a muffin tin (pan). On a floured surface, form the dough into a flattened sausage 10cm/4in wide. Press the blueberries into the surface.

3 Cut the dough into 10 pieces. Using floured hands, form each into a ball, then press into a muffin cup. Mix the milk and egg yolk in a bowl. Brush thinly over the muffins. Slash the tops twice with a knife.

4 Preheat the oven to 220°C/425°F/Gas 7. Leave the dough in a warm place for 15 minutes, then bake for 13–15 minutes until golden and risen. Turn the muffins out on to a floured tray and leave to cool. Serve fresh.

Nutritional information per portion: Energy 302kcal/1266kJ; Protein 6g; Carbohydrate 33.5g, of which sugars 7.1g; Fat 17g, of which saturates 10.2g; Cholesterol 117mg; Calcium 145mg; Fibre 1.3g; Sodium 288mg.

Brioche breakfast with hot fudge

Brioche and ice cream is an unexpected pairing, but an absolutely divine one for a lazy breakfast with friends. The hot fudge sauce is added for sheer indulgence.

SERVES 2

2 individual brioches
**2 huge scoops of best vanilla or coffee ice
   cream**

FOR THE HOT FUDGE SAUCE
**50g/2oz best dark (bittersweet) chocolate
   with 70% cocoa solids**

15g/¹⁄₂oz/1 tbsp butter
30ml/2 tbsp golden (light corn) syrup
**150g/5oz/scant 1 cup soft light brown sugar,
   sifted**
5ml/1 tsp vanilla extract

1 Set the oven to 200°C/400°F/Gas 6 and, while it is heating, make the hot fudge sauce. Break up the chocolate and put the pieces into a bowl placed over a pan of barely simmering water. Leave undisturbed for about 10 minutes until the chocolate is completely melted, then stir in the butter.

2 Add 75ml/5 tbsp boiling water to the chocolate and butter, stir well to blend, then stir in the syrup, sugar and vanilla extract. Pour and scrape into a pan and bring to the boil, then turn down the heat and allow to barely bubble for 5 minutes.

3 Meanwhile, put the brioches on a baking sheet and warm them in the oven for 5 minutes. Herein lies the secret to this dish: warm the brioches so that they are slightly crisp on the outside but soft, fluffy and warm on the inside.

4 After 5 minutes, remove the pan of sauce from the heat. Immediately split the brioches open and gently pull out a little of the insides. Generously fill each brioche base with ice cream and gently press on the tops.

5 Put into serving bowls or on to plates and pour over the hot fudge sauce. Serve immediately. (Any leftover fudge sauce can be stored in a jar in the refrigerator to melt at a moment's notice.)

Nutritional information per portion: Energy 913kcal/3853kj; Protein 13.8g; Carbohydrate 163.3g, of which sugars 121.5g; Fat 27.2g, of which saturates 15.4g; Cholesterol 18mg; Calcium 257mg; Fibre 3g; Sodium 674mg.

Pain au chocolat

A freshly baked pain au chocolat is almost impossible to resist, with its buttery, flaky yet crisp pastry concealing a delectable chocolate filling. For a special finish, drizzle melted chocolate over the tops of the freshly baked and cooked pastries.

MAKES 9

250g/9oz/2¼ cups unbleached white bread flour
30ml/2 tbsp skimmed milk powder (non fat dry milk)
15ml/1 tbsp caster (superfine) sugar
2.5ml/½ tsp salt
7.5ml/1½ tsp easy-blend (rapid-rise) dried yeast

140g/5oz/⅔ cup butter, softened
125ml/4½fl oz/generous ½ cup hand-hot water
225g/8oz plain (semisweet) chocolate, broken into pieces

FOR THE GLAZE
1 egg yolk
15ml/1 tbsp full cream (whole) milk

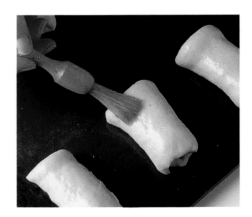

1 Mix the flour, milk powder, sugar and salt in a bowl. Stir in the yeast and make a well in the middle of these dry ingredients. Melt 25g/1oz/2 tbsp of the butter and add it to the dry ingredients, pouring it into the well in the middle of the mixture. Pour in the water and then mix to form a firm dough.

2 Turn the dough out on to a lightly floured surface and knead it thoroughly for about 10 minutes, until it is smooth and elastic. When pressed on the surface it should spring back rather than retain the dent.

3 Dust the bowl with flour and return the dough to it. Cover with clear film (plastic wrap) and leave in a warm place until doubled in size. Meanwhile shape the remaining softened butter into an oblong block, about 2cm/¾in thick.

5 Lightly grease two baking sheets. When the dough has doubled in size, turn it out on to a floured surface. Knock back (punch down) and shape into a ball. Cut a cross halfway through the top.

6 Roll out around the cross, leaving a risen centre. Place the butter in the centre. Fold the rolled dough over the butter to enclose; seal the edges.

7 Roll to a rectangle 2cm/¾in thick, twice as long as wide. Fold the bottom third up and the top down; seal the edges with a rolling pin. Wrap in lightly oiled clear film. Place in the refrigerator and chill for 20 minutes. Do the same again twice more, giving a quarter turn and chilling each time. Chill again for 30 minutes.

8 Roll out the dough to a rectangle measuring 52 x 30cm/21 x 12in. Using a sharp knife, cut the dough into three strips lengthways and widthways to make nine 18 x 10cm/7 x 4in rectangles.

9 Divide the chocolate among the three dough rectangles, placing the pieces lengthways at one short end. Mix the egg yolk and milk for the glaze together. Brush the mixture over the edges of the dough. Roll up each piece of dough to completely enclose the chocolate, then press the edges together to seal.

10 Place the pastries seam side down on the prepared baking sheets. Cover with oiled clear film and leave to rise in a warm place for about 30 minutes or until doubled in size.

11 Meanwhile, preheat the oven to 200°C/400°F/Gas 6. Brush the pastries with the remaining glaze and bake for about 15 minutes, or until golden. Turn out on to a wire rack to cool just slightly and serve warm.

Nutritional information per pain au chocolat: Energy 345kcal/1441kJ; Protein 4g; Carbohydrate 39.3g, of which sugars 17.9g; Fat 20.1g, of which saturates 12.4g; Cholesterol 35mg; Calcium 51mg; Fibre 1.5g; Sodium 206mg.

Warm pancakes with caramelized pears

If you can find them, use Williams pears for this recipe because they are juicier than most other varieties. For a real breakfast treat, top with a spoonful of crème fraîche or fromage frais.

SERVES 4

8 ready-made pancakes

**4 ripe pears, peeled, cored and thickly
  sliced**

**30ml/2 tbsp light muscovado (brown)
  sugar**

50g/2oz/¼ cup butter

1 Preheat the oven to 150°C/ 330°F/Gas 2. Tightly wrap the pancakes in foil and place in the oven to warm through.

2 Heat the butter in a large frying pan and add the pears. Fry for 2–3 minutes, until the undersides are golden. Turn the pears over and sprinkle with sugar. Cook for 2–3 minutes, or until the sugar dissolves and the pan juices become sticky.

3 Remove the pancakes from the oven and take them out of the foil. Divide the pears among the pancakes, positioning them in one quarter.

4 Fold each pancake in half over the filling, then into quarters and place two folded pancakes on each serving plate. Drizzle over any remaining juices and serve immediately.

Nutritional information per portion: Energy 544kcal/2274kJ; Protein 7.7g; Carbohydrate 64.9g, of which sugars 42.4g; Fat 29.9g, of which saturates 6.5g; Cholesterol 27mg; Calcium 155mg; Fibre 4.3g; Sodium 144mg.

Egg pancakes

A quick way of making pancakes is to use eggs as a raising agent. When adding more milk, these can be baked thinly to use as a dessert, and can be eaten with sugar, jam or ice cream.

MAKES 25

400g/14oz/3¼ cups
   plain (all-purpose) flour
5 eggs
1 egg yolk
5ml/1 tsp salt
750ml/1¼ pints/3 cups full cream
   (whole) milk
25g/1oz/2 tbsp butter

1 Sift the flour into a bowl and make a well. Add the eggs, egg yolk and salt, mix the eggs and stir, gradually incorporating the flour.

2 Add half the milk and beat with a hand-held electric mixer to make a smooth thick batter. Stir in the remaining milk. Cover and leave to rest in the refrigerator for 30 minutes.

3 Melt the butter in a 20cm/8in non-stick frying pan, and stir it into the batter.

4 Re-heat the pan and cook the pancakes as described opposite, but without adding any further butter.

Nutritional information per pancake: Energy 93kcal/392kJ; Protein 3.9g; Carbohydrate 13.8g, of which sugars 1.7g; Fat 2.9g, of which saturates 1.2g; Cholesterol 50mg; Calcium 65mg; Fibre 0.5g; Sodium 112mg.

Griddled tomatoes on soda bread

Nothing could be simpler than this delightful appetizer, yet a drizzle of olive oil and balsamic vinegar and shavings of Parmesan cheese transform it into something really rather special.

SERVES 4

olive oil, for brushing and drizzling
6 tomatoes, thickly sliced
4 thick slices soda bread
balsamic vinegar, for drizzling
salt and ground black pepper
shavings of Parmesan cheese, to serve

1 Brush a griddle pan with olive oil and heat. Add the tomato slices and cook for about 4 minutes, turning once, until softened and slightly blackened. Or, heat the grill (broiler) to high and line the rack with foil. Grill (broil) the slices for 4–6 minutes, turning once, until softened.

2 Meanwhile, lightly toast the soda bread. Place the tomatoes on top of the toast and then drizzle each portion with a little olive oil and balsamic vinegar. Season to taste with salt and black pepper and serve immediately with thin shavings of Parmesan cheese.

Nutritional information per portion: Energy 172kcal/724kJ; Protein 4g; Carbohydrate 25.1g, of which sugars 5.8g; Fat 6.9g, of which saturates 0.9g; Cholesterol 0mg; Calcium 63mg; Fibre 2.3g; Sodium 171mg.

Drop scones with bacon and maple syrup

Also known as Scotch pancakes, drop scones are available in most supermarkets. You can use golden syrup or jam to serve, or slices of soft cheese for a more savoury mixture.

SERVES 4

8 ready-made Scotch pancakes
**8 dry-cured smoked back (lean) bacon
  rashers (strips)**
30ml/2 tbsp maple syrup

1 Preheat the oven to 150°C/
330°F/Gas 2. Wrap the pancakes in
a sheet of foil and place them in the
oven to warm through.

2 Meanwhile, preheat the grill
(broiler) and arrange the bacon on a
grill pan. Grill (broil) for 3–4 minutes
on each side, until crisp.

3 Divide the warm pancakes
between four warmed serving plates
and top with the grilled bacon
rashers. Drizzle with the maple
syrup and serve immediately.

Nutritional information per portion: Energy 417kcal1750kJ; Protein 27g; Carbohydrate 36g, of which sugars 2g; Fat 19g, of which saturates 11g; Cholesterol 73mg; Calcium 498mg; Fibre 1.1g; Sodium 1.1mg.

Croissants with scrambled eggs, caviar and pancetta

This classic combination relies on very fresh eggs and very buttery croissants. Crème fraîche adds a little bite while the pancetta contributes a crunchy smokiness.

SERVES 4

4 croissants
50g/2oz/¼ cup butter
12 thin smoked pancetta or streaky (fatty)
   bacon rashers (strips)
8 eggs, at room temperature

60ml/4 tbsp crème fraîche
60ml/4 tbsp Avruga or Keta caviar
45ml/3 tbsp chopped fresh chives
salt and ground black pepper

1 Preheat the oven to 200°C/400°F/Gas 6. Place the croissants on a baking tray and warm them in the oven for about 5 minutes, then switch the oven off.

2 Melt the butter in a non-stick frying pan until foaming, then add the pancetta or bacon. Cook over a high heat until very crisp. Lift out on to a plate and keep warm in the oven with the croissants. Leave the butter and fat in the pan and reheat gently.

3 Lightly beat the eggs with the crème fraîche and season with salt and pepper. Split the croissants in half and place on warmed plates. Pour the eggs into the pan and stir with a wooden spoon. Cook over a low heat, stirring slowly, until the mixture is creamy and thick. Remove the pan from the heat.

4 Fill the croissants with the scrambled eggs, spoon over the caviar or put it to one side and lay the pancetta on top. Be a little adventurous with the presentation – it makes all the difference, especially when the ingredients are so special. It is said that we eat with the eyes first, then the mouth. Setting the bacon so that it points skywards gives the whole thing a distinctly cheeky look, and an extra spoonful of real caviar on the side looks truly decadent – keep the jar handy for seconds. Sprinkle with chopped chives and serve immediately.

Nutritional information per portion: Energy 668kcal/2860kJ; Protein 27g; Carbohydrate 31g, of which sugars 5g; Fat 51g, of which saturates 25g; Cholesterol 578mg; Calcium 88mg; Fibre 2.0g; Sodium 1297mg.

Bubble and squeak

Whether you have leftovers, or cook this old-fashioned classic from fresh, be sure to give it a really good "squeak" (fry) in the pan so it turns a rich deep brown and becomes deliciously crunchy.

SERVES 4

60ml/4 tbsp dripping, bacon fat or vegetable
oil
1 onion, finely chopped
450g/1lb floury potatoes, cooked and
mashed

225g/8oz cooked cabbage or Brussels
sprouts, finely chopped
salt and ground black pepper

1 Heat 30ml/2 tbsp of the dripping, fat or oil in a heavy-based frying pan. Add the onion and cook, stirring frequently, until softened but not browned.

2 In a large bowl, mix together the potatoes and cooked cabbage or sprouts and season with salt and plenty of pepper to taste.

3 Add the vegetables to the pan with the cooked onions, stir well, then press the vegetable mixture into a large, even cake. Cook over a medium heat for about 15 minutes until the cake is browned underneath.

4 Invert a large plate over the pan, and, holding it tightly against the pan, turn them both over together. Lift off the frying pan, return it to the heat and add the remaining dripping fat or oil. When hot, slide the cake back into the pan, browned side uppermost.

5 Cook over a medium heat for 10 minutes or until golden brown. Serve hot, in wedges.

COOK'S TIP
If you don't have leftover cooked cabbage or Brussels sprouts, shred raw cabbage and cook with Brussels sprouts in boiling salted water until tender. Drain, then chop.

Nutritional information per portion: Energy 205kcal/857kJ; Protein 3.5g; Carbohydrate 23.3g, of which sugars 4.2g; Fat 11.5g, of which saturates 1.2g; Cholesterol 0mg; Calcium 34mg; Fibre 3g; Sodium 15mg.

Smoked salmon and cream cheese bagel

'Lox' comes from laks, *the Yiddish word for smoked salmon, and this recipe is a Jewish deli classic. Be generous with the smoked salmon, use the best cream cheese and always warm the bagels.*

SERVES 2

2 bagels
115–175g/4–6oz/¹/₂–³/₄ cup full-fat
    cream cheese
150g/5oz sliced best
    smoked salmon
ground black pepper
lemon wedges

1 Preheat the oven to 200°C/ 400°F/Gas 6. Put the bagels on a large baking sheet and warm them in the oven for 4–5 minutes.

2 Remove the bagels from the oven, split them in two and spread the bottom halves with cream cheese.

3 Pile the salmon on top and grind over plenty of black pepper.

4 Squeeze over some lemon juice, then top with the other bagel half and eat while still warm.

COOK'S TIP
For an elegant touch, place a wedge of lemon in the centre of a square of muslin (cheesecloth), bring up the edges, tie with fine string and put it on the plate. The lemon can now be squeezed without a pip shooting into your eye.

Nutritional information per bagel: Energy 375kcal/1571kJ; Protein 25g; Carbohydrate 28.9g, of which sugars 3.3g; Fat 18.6g, of which saturates 9.5g; Cholesterol 55mg; Calcium 44mg; Fibre 1.2g; Sodium 1775mg.

Smoked salmon and chive omelette

The addition of chopped smoked salmon gives a luxurious finish to this simple dish. You could replace the salmon and chives with chopped ham and parsley or grated Cheddar and basil.

SERVES 2

4 eggs
15ml/1 tbsp chopped fresh chives
50g/2oz smoked salmon, roughly chopped
a knob (pat) of butter
salt and ground black pepper

1 Beat the eggs until just combined, then stir in the chives and season with salt and pepper.

2 Heat the butter in a medium-sized pan until foamy. Pour in the eggs and cook over a medium heat for 3–4 minutes, drawing the egg from around the edge into the centre of the pan from time to time.

3 At this stage of preparation, you can either leave the top of the omelette slightly soft or finish it off under the grill (broiler), depending on how you prefer to eat your omelette.

4 Top with the smoked salmon, fold the omelette over and cut in half to serve.

Nutritional information per portion: Energy 221kcal/920kJ; Protein 19g; Carbohydrate 0.2g, of which sugars 0.2g; Fat 16.4g, of which saturates 5.9g; Cholesterol 400mg; Calcium 65mg; Fibre 0.1g; Sodium 641mg.

Kedgeree

This traditional Scottish and English dish using smoked fish became popular for breakfast or high tea. It is a convenient recipe to use when preparing breakfast for a large group of people.

SERVES 4–6

450g/1lb smoked haddock
300ml/¹⁄₂ pint/1¹⁄₄ cups full cream
    (whole) milk
175g/6oz/scant 1 cup long grain rice
a pinch of freshly grated nutmeg and
    cayenne pepper
50g/2oz/¹⁄₄ cup butter
1 onion, peeled and finely chopped
2 hard-boiled eggs
salt and ground black pepper
chopped fresh parsley, to garnish
lemon wedges and wholemeal
    (whole-wheat) toast, to serve

1 Poach the haddock in the milk by cooking at simmering point, made up with enough water to cover the fish, for about 8 minutes, or until just cooked. Skin the haddock, remove the bones and flake the flesh. Set aside.

2 Bring 600ml/1 pint/2¹⁄₂ cups water to the boil. Add the rice, cover with a lid and cook over a low heat for about 25 minutes, or until all the water has been absorbed. Season with salt, black pepper, nutmeg and cayenne pepper.

3 Heat 15g/¹⁄₂oz/1 tbsp butter in a pan and fry the onion until soft. Set aside. Chop one of the hard-boiled eggs, and cut the other into wedges.

4 Stir the remaining butter into the rice and add the flaked haddock, onion and the chopped egg. Season to taste and heat the mixture through gently. To serve, pile up the kedgeree on a warmed dish, sprinkle generously with parsley and arrange the wedges of egg on top. Put the lemon wedges around the base and serve hot with the toast.

Nutritional information per portion: Energy 399kcal/1668kJ; Protein 28.9g; Carbohydrate 38g, of which sugars 2.2g; Fat 14.6g, of which saturates 7.6g; Cholesterol 181mg; Calcium 62mg; Fibre 0.5g; Sodium 974mg.

Eggs bénédict

This dish consists of two halves of an English muffin, loaded with ham or bacon, and poached eggs and Hollandaise. While straightforward, every element needs to be perfectly executed.

SERVES 2

2 large (US extra large) eggs, chilled
4 Ayrshire bacon rashers (strips) or
   unsmoked rolled pancetta (the circular
   shape fits the muffin perfectly)
2 English muffins or 4 crumpets
butter

FOR THE QUICK HOLLANDAISE
2 large (US extra large) egg yolks, beaten
10ml/2 tsp lemon juice
10ml/2 tsp tarragon wine vinegar
115g/4oz/1/2 cup butter
15ml/1 tbsp chopped fresh tarragon
salt and ground black pepper

1 Bring a pan of water almost to the boil. Crack each egg into a cup and slide it into the water. Allow the water to tremble (not boil), for 1 minute. Remove the pan from the heat and allow the eggs to sit for 10 minutes.

2 Meanwhile, grill (broil) the bacon or pancetta until crisp. Keep it warm. Split and toast the muffins, or toast the crumpets, and butter generously; keep warm.

3 Make the hollandaise. Season the yolks, beat and put into a food processor or blender. Put the lemon juice and vinegar into a pan and heat until it boils. With the blender or beater running, pour the hot liquid on to the eggs.

4 Melt the butter until foaming. With the machine running, pour the butter on to the eggs in a stream. Add the tarragon. Thin the hollandaise by beating in a little warm water. Lift the poached eggs out with a slotted spoon and drain. Sit a toasted muffin on a warm plate, top with bacon and put an egg on top. Spoon the hollandaise over the top and eat immediately.

Nutritional information per portion: Energy 553kcal/2304kJ; Protein 19.8g; Carbohydrate 31.6g, of which sugars 2.2g; Fat 39.7g, of which saturates 18.9g; Cholesterol 427mg; Calcium 148mg; Fibre 1.3g; Sodium 635mg.

Brandade of smoked mackerel with finger toasts

The original French version of this dish, brandade de morue, is a warm potato, salt cod, olive oil and garlic purée, and is supremely soothing. This uses smoked mackerel rather than salt cod.

SERVES 6

450g/1lb peppered smoked mackerel
   fillets, with skin on
225ml/7½ fl oz/scant 1 cup full cream
   (whole) milk
225ml/7½ fl oz/scant 1 cup water
a sprig of fresh thyme
1 bay leaf
450g/1lb floury potatoes, peeled
150ml/¼ pint/⅔ cup half olive and half
   sunflower oil
15ml/1 tbsp horseradish sauce
30ml/2 tbsp wholegrain mustard
45ml/3 tbsp chopped fresh parsley
15ml/1 tbsp chopped fresh tarragon
ground black pepper
extra virgin olive oil, for serving

FOR THE FINGER TOASTS

6 slices day-old, good white bread
115g/4oz/½ cup butter, melted

1 Preheat the oven to 180°C/350°F/ Gas 4. Cut the crusts off the bread and brush both sides with butter. Cut into fingers and spread on a baking sheet. Bake for 15–20 minutes until golden and crisp. Keep warm.

2 Place the smoked mackerel fillets in a large pan with the milk, water, thyme and bay leaf. Bring almost to the boil, remove from the heat and let cool.

3 In a separate pan, boil the potatoes for about 20 minutes until tender, then mash well. Keep warm. Strain the liquid from the mackerel and reserve. Remove the skin from the fish and flake the flesh.

4 Heat the oils in a large, deep pan until a piece of bread sizzles when added. Add a spoonful of fish and beat with an electric whisk on slow. Keep adding the fish over a medium heat, beating until it has all been added.

5 Stir in the horseradish, mustard and herbs, then beat in the mashed potato. Beat in enough cooking liquid to give a smooth, creamy consistency. Season. Pile into a dish and drizzle with olive oil before serving with the finger toasts.

Nutritional information per portion: Energy 881kcal/3369kJ; Protein 21g; Carbohydrate 33g, of which sugars 4g; Fat 67g, of which saturates 19g; Cholesterol 125mg; Calcium 117mg; Fibre 2.6g; Sodium 993mg.

Black pudding snackettes

This is a trendy take on that breakfast favourite, fried black pudding. Make it with black pudding or morcilla – the Spanish black pudding seasoned with garlic and oregano. Be sure to make plenty.

SERVES 4

15ml/1 tbsp olive oil
1 onion, thinly sliced
2 garlic cloves, thinly sliced
5ml/1 tsp dried oregano
5ml/1 tsp paprika
225g/8oz black pudding (blood sausage),
    cut into 12 thick slices
1 thin French stick, sliced into 12
30ml/2 tbsp fino sherry
sugar, to taste
salt and ground black pepper
sprigs of fresh oregano, to garnish

1 Heat the olive oil in a large frying pan and fry the sliced onion, garlic, oregano and paprika for 7–8 minutes until the onion is softened and has turned golden brown.

2 Add the slices of black pudding, then increase the heat and cook them for 2 minutes, without stirring. Turn them over carefully with a spatula and cook for a further 3 minutes until crisp.

3 Arrange the rounds of bread on a large serving plate and top each with a slice of black pudding. Stir the sherry into the onions and add a little sugar to taste. Heat, swirling the mixture around the pan until bubbling, then season with salt and black pepper.

4 Spoon a little of the onion mixture on top of each slice of black pudding. Sprinkle the oregano over and serve.

Nutritional information per portion: Energy 513kcal/2164kJ; Protein 16.2g; Carbohydrate 77.4g, of which sugars 4.8g; Fat 16.7g, of which saturates 5.1g; Cholesterol 24mg; Calcium 213mg; Fibre 3.2g; Sodium 1208mg.

Full English breakfast

For most of us, a cooked breakfast is a special treat, harking back to the 19th century when the buffet tables of the rich groaned with food. As well as bacon, sausages and eggs there might have been fish, kedgeree, potatoes, kidneys, chops, steaks, cold meats and devilled chicken or pheasant.

SERVES 4

225–250g/8–9oz small potatoes
vegetable oil, for grilling and frying
butter, for grilling and frying
4 large or 8 small good-quality
    sausages

8 rashers (strips) of back or streaky (fatty)
    bacon, preferably dry-cured
4 tomatoes
4 small slices of bread, crusts removed
4 eggs

1 Thinly slice the potatoes. Heat 15ml/1 tbsp oil with a knob of butter in a large, preferably non-stick frying pan, add the potatoes and cook over a medium heat for 10–15 minutes, turning them occasionally until they are crisp, golden, and cooked through.

2 Using a slotted spoon, lift the potatoes out of the pan and keep them warm on a dish in a low oven.

3 Meanwhile, grill or fry the sausages in a little oil until golden brown all over and cooked through (test by inserting a skewer in the centre – the juices should run clear). Keep warm.

4 Grill the bacon or fry it in a little oil in the non-stick pan. Keep warm. Halve the tomatoes and either top each half with a tiny piece of butter and grill until they are soft and bubbling, or fry in a little oil in the frying pan. Keep warm.

5 Fry the bread in a little oil and butter over a medium-high heat until crisp and golden brown. Keep warm.

6 Add extra oil if necessary to the hot frying pan. As soon as the oil is hot, crack the eggs into the pan, leaving space between them. Cook over a medium heat, spooning the hot fat over occasionally to set the yolks, until cooked to your liking. When the eggs are cooked, arrange the ingredients on warmed plates and serve immediately.

Nutritional information per portion: Energy 731kcal/3046kJ; Protein 32.7g; Carbohydrate 35.3g, of which sugars 7.6g; Fat 52.2g, of which saturates 16.5g; Cholesterol 288mg; Calcium 185mg; Fibre 3.1g; Sodium 2049mg.

Sustaining Lunches

When it comes to lunchtime in the comfort zone, the order of the day is food that can be easily rustled up from fresh and yummy ingredients and can be eaten with a minimum of fuss and maximum enjoyment. This chapter includes dishes ranging from a soothing and nutritious old-fashioned chicken soup to grilled toast with goat's cheese and beetroot, and the creamy delight of cheese and onion flan.

Tomato soup with black olive ciabatta toasts

Tomato soup is everybody's favourite, particularly when made with fresh sun-ripened tomatoes. This delicious soup is wonderfully warming and has an earthy richness.

SERVES 6

450g/1lb very ripe fresh tomatoes
30ml/2 tbsp olive oil
1 onion, chopped
1 garlic clove, crushed
30ml/2 tbsp sherry vinegar
30ml/2 tbsp tomato purée (paste)
15ml/1 tbsp cornflour (cornstarch) or
   potato flour
300ml/$\frac{1}{2}$ pint/1$\frac{1}{4}$ cups passata
   (bottled strained tomatoes)
1 bay leaf
900ml/1$\frac{1}{2}$ pints/3$\frac{3}{4}$ cups vegetable or
   chicken stock
200ml/7fl oz/scant 1 cup crème fraîche
salt and ground black pepper
basil leaves, to garnish

**FOR THE BLACK OLIVE
CIABATTA TOASTS**

1 plain or black olive ciabatta
1 small red (bell) pepper
3 whole garlic cloves, skins on
225g/8oz black olives (preferably
   a wrinkly Greek variety)
30–45ml/2–3 tbsp salted capers or
   capers in vinegar
12 drained canned anchovy fillets or
   1 small can tuna in oil, drained
about 150ml/$\frac{1}{4}$ pint/$\frac{2}{3}$ cup extra virgin
   olive oil
fresh lemon juice and ground black
   pepper, to taste
45ml/3 tbsp chopped fresh basil

1 Make the toasts first. Preheat the oven to 200°C/400°F/Gas 6. Split the ciabatta in half and cut each half into nine pieces. Place on a baking sheet and bake for 10–15 minutes until crisp.

2 Place the whole pepper and garlic cloves under a hot grill (broiler) and cook for 15 minutes, turning, until charred all over. If you prefer, you can bake them in the oven for about 25 minutes. Once charred, put the garlic and pepper in a plastic bag, seal and leave to cool for 10 minutes.

3 Peel off the pepper skin and remove the stalk and seeds. Peel the skin off the garlic. Stone (pit) the olives. Rinse the capers. Place the ingredients in a food processor or blender with the anchovies or tuna and process until roughly chopped.

4 With the machine running, slowly add the olive oil until you have a fairly smooth dark paste. Alternatively, just stir in the olive oil. Season to taste with lemon juice and pepper. Stir in the basil.

5 Spread the paste on the finger toasts, or, if not using immediately, transfer to a jar, cover with a layer of olive oil and keep in the refrigerator for up to three weeks.

6 For the soup, cut the tomatoes in half and remove the seeds and pulp using a lemon squeezer. Press the pulp through a sieve (strainer) and reserve the liquid.

7 Heat the oil in a pan and add the onion, garlic, sherry vinegar, tomato purée and the tomato halves. Stir, then cover the pan and cook over a low heat for 1 hour, stirring occasionally. When done, process the soup in a food processor or blender. Pass through a sieve then return to the pan.

8 Mix the cornflour or potato flour with the reserved tomato pulp. Stir into the soup with the passata, bay leaf and stock. Simmer for 30 minutes. Stir in the crème fraîche and garnish with the basil leaves. Serve piping hot, with the ciabatta toasts.

Nutritional information per portion: Energy 532kcal/2211kJ; Protein 11.9g; Carbohydrate 29.3g, of which sugars 7.6g; Fat 41.7g, of which saturates 13.2g; Cholesterol 50mg; Calcium 120mg; Fibre 3.5g; Sodium 1352mg.

Onion soup

Believed to be a good remedy for a hangover, onion soup is certainly a comforting winter warmer.
This recipe is Belgian and cooks here prepare it sprinkled with Gruyère or Parmesan.

SERVES 4–6

50g/2oz/¼ cup butter

4 medium onions (total weight about
    800g/1¾lb), chopped

4 garlic cloves, finely chopped

1 medium potato (about 200g/7oz),
    peeled and chopped

45ml/3 tbsp sherry or Calvados

1 litre/1¾ pints/4 cups vegetable,
    chicken or beef stock

1–2 sprigs fresh thyme

1 bay leaf

salt and ground black pepper

45ml/3 tbsp freshly chopped parsley, to
    garnish

freshly grated Gruyère cheese (optional)

hearty country bread or croûtons, to
    serve

1 Melt the butter in a large pan and sauté the onions over medium high heat for about 10 minutes or until lightly caramelized. Add the garlic and sauté for 1 minute more.

2 Add the potato to the onions and stir. Add the sherry or Calvados and let the mixture simmer for 3 minutes more.

3 Pour in the stock and add the thyme and bay leaf. Bring to the boil, reduce the heat and simmer for 35 minutes.

4 Remove the herbs and purée with a hand-held blender or in a food processor, until it reaches the desired consistency.

5 Season with salt and ground black pepper, to taste. Reheat if necessary, then ladle the soup into bowls.

6 Top each serving with freshly chopped parsley and add grated cheese if you like. Serve immediately with hearty country bread or croûtons.

Nutritional information per portion: Energy 146kcal/608kJ; Protein 2.5g; Carbohydrate 16.3g, of which sugars 8.1g; Fat 7.5g, of which saturates 4.4g; Cholesterol 18mg; Calcium 38mg; Fibre 2.2g; Sodium 339mg.

Smoked haddock chowder

This soup originates from Cullen, a fishing village in Scotland, and is traditionally made with Finnan haddock that has been cold-smoked until it is just the palest gold in colour.

SERVES 4

900g/2lb undyed smoked haddock, preferably Finnan

1 onion, finely sliced

450ml/³/₄ pint/scant 2 cups full cream (whole) milk

450ml/³/₄ pint/scant 2 cups water

450g/1lb floury potatoes, peeled and cut into large chunks

225g/8oz leeks, finely sliced

300ml/¹/₂ pint/1¹/₄ cups single (light) cream

1 large (US extra large) egg yolk

30ml/2 tbsp chopped fresh parsley

50g/2oz/¹/₄ cup butter

salt and ground black pepper

1 Put the haddock, skin-side up, in a shallow pan and cover with the onion slices, milk and water. Bring the liquid to just below boiling point, turn down the heat and poach gently for about 10 minutes until cooked – it should flake easily.

2 Meanwhile, boil the potatoes in salted water for 10–15 minutes, or until tender, then drain and mash.

3 When the fish is cooked, strain the cooking liquid into a pan and reserve. Flake the fish and set aside.

4 Whisk the mashed potato into the reserved fish liquid, stir in the leeks, bring to the boil and simmer for 10 minutes until the leeks are tender.

5 Whisk the cream and egg yolk and stir into the soup. Reheat gently until slightly thickened. Gently stir in the flaked fish, taste, adjust the seasoning, and heat through.

6 Stir the parsley into the soup and serve piping hot, dotted with knobs (pats) of butter that will melt and run over the surface of the soup.

Nutritional information per portion: Energy 205kcal/864kJ; Protein 16.1g; Carbohydrate 19g, of which sugars 6.4g; Fat 7.8g, of which saturates 4.7g; Cholesterol 41mg; Calcium 137mg; Fibre 1g; Sodium 132mg.

Old-fashioned chicken soup

A real chicken soup, clear, golden and warming, filled with lightly cooked pasta, is not called Jewish penicillin for nothing – it really warms you up and it feels as if it is actually doing you good. This dish is one to bring steaming to the table in a big white soup tureen. It does takes a little time to make, but this recipe never fails to be appreciated.

SERVES 4–6

2kg/4½lb boiling fowl (stewing chicken) with giblets (except liver), or same weight of guinea fowl and chicken wings and thighs, mixed

1 large onion, halved

2 large carrots, halved lengthways

6 celery sticks, roughly chopped

1 bay leaf

175g/6oz vermicelli pasta

45ml/3 tbsp chopped fresh parsley or whole parsley leaves

salt and ground black pepper

1 Put the chicken, or guinea fowl and chicken pieces, into a large pan with all the vegetables and the bay leaf. Cover with 2.4 litres/4 pints/10 cups cold water. Bring slowly to the boil, carefully skimming off any scum that rises to the top. Add 5ml/1 tsp salt and some ground black pepper.

2 Turn down the heat and simmer the soup slowly for at least 2 hours, or until the fowl is tender. When simmering, the surface of the liquid should just tremble. If it boils, the soup will be cloudy.

3 When tender, remove the bird from the broth and strip the flesh off the carcass. (Use the meat in sandwiches or a risotto.) Return the bones to the soup and simmer gently for another hour.

4 Strain the soup into a bowl, cool, then chill overnight.

5 The next day the soup should have set to a solid jelly and will be covered with a thin layer of solidified chicken fat. Carefully remove the fat. To serve the soup, reheat in a large pan. Add the vermicelli and chopped parsley, and simmer for 6–8 minutes until the pasta is cooked. Taste and season well. Serve piping hot.

Nutritional information per portion: Energy 176kcal/748kJ; Protein 6.3g; Carbohydrate 37.5g, of which sugars 5.7g; Fat 1.2g, of which saturates 0.1g; Cholesterol 0mg; Calcium 66mg; Fibre 3.4g; Sodium 39mg.

Fried mozzarella sandwich

This is reassuring snacking Italian style, with glorious melting mozzarella in crisp fried egg-soaked bread. The result is a delicious savoury sandwich.

SERVES 2

115g/4oz mozzarella cheese, thickly
    sliced
4 thick slices white bread
1 egg
30ml/2 tbsp full cream (whole) milk
vegetable oil, for frying
salt and freshly ground black pepper
tomato wedges and fresh basil sprigs,
    to garnish

1 Place the cheese on two slices of bread and season to taste. Top with the bread to make two sandwiches.

2 Beat the egg with the milk. Season to taste and pour into a shallow dish.

3 Dip the sandwiches into the egg and milk mixture until coated.

4 Leave to soak while heating the oil in a large, heavy frying pan.

5 Fry the sandwiches, in batches if necessary, until golden brown and crisp on both sides.

6 Remove from the frying pan and drain well on kitchen paper. Garnish with tomato and basil.

VARIATIONS
Use any favourite cheese instead of mozzarella. Add some chopped spring onions (scallions) and sliced cooked ham or salami before sandwiching the bread together.

Nutritional information per portion: Energy 429kcal/1789kJ; Protein 18.9g; Carbohydrate 30.5g, of which sugars 2.7g; Fat 26.6g, of which saturates 10.4g; Cholesterol 129mg; Calcium 331mg; Fibre 1.9g; Sodium 539mg.

Grilled goat's cheese with baby beetroot

Beetroots are considered a delicacy when they are freshly dug out of the ground in early summer. In this recipe the goat's cheese marries well with the sweetness of the beetroot.

SERVES 6

6 small raw beetroots (beets)
6 slices French bread
6 slices (250g/9oz) goat's cheese
30ml/2 tbsp walnut oil
salt and ground black pepper

1 Cook the beetroots in boiling salted water for 40 minutes until tender. Leave to cool then remove the skin and slice the beetroots.

2 Toast the French bread on both sides. Arrange the beetroot in a fan on the toasted bread then put a slice of goat's cheese on top.

3 Place all the bread slices on a grill (broiler) pan and grill (broil) until the cheese has melted and is golden brown.

4 Serve immediately, drizzled with a little walnut oil and black pepper ground on top.

Nutritional information per portion: Energy 290kcal/1215kJ; Protein 13.3g; Carbohydrate 26.7g, of which sugars 5g; Fat 15.2g, of which saturates 7.9g; Cholesterol 39mg; Calcium 114mg; Fibre 1.9g; Sodium 530mg.

Classic egg mayo sandwich with mustard and cress

When the egg is perfectly hard-boiled, the mayonnaise freshly made and the bread soft and crusty, this is one of the most satisfying sandwiches to eat.

SERVES 2

4 eggs
4 spring onions (scallions), chopped
1 fat dill-pickled cucumber, roughly chopped
softened butter, for spreading
4 thick slices bread, freshly cut from a crusty
   multigrain or malted grain loaf
mustard and cress, watercress, or rocket
   (arugula)
salt and ground black pepper

FOR THE MAYONNAISE
2 egg yolks
2.5ml/¹/₂ tsp Dijon or English (hot) mustard
300ml/¹/₂ pint/1¹/₄ cups mild olive oil
15ml/1 tbsp white wine vinegar or a squeeze
   of lemon juice
salt and ground black pepper

1 First make the mayonnaise. Remember that all the ingredients should be at room temperature to ensure the mixture doesn't curdle. Beat the egg yolks with the mustard and salt in a small bowl.

2 Add a tablespoon of oil, then, using an electric whisk or a balloon whisk (though using this will give you a serious arm-ache), whisk until the mixture begins to thicken. Add another spoonful and whisk well again until thickened. Repeat this process until you've used half the oil. Beat well, then add the vinegar or lemon juice and beat again.

3 Now add the rest of the oil in a thin, steady stream, beating all the time, until all the oil is added and the mayonnaise is nice and thick. Add salt and pepper to taste. (At this stage you can flavour the mayonnaise with ingredients such as curry paste or powder, herbs, spices, mustard or wasabi paste.) Cover and store in the refrigerator until needed.

4 To hard-boil the eggs, place them in a pan and cover with cold water. Bring the water to simmering point, then simmer for 7 minutes. Immediately pour off the boiling water, set the pan in the sink and fill with cold water. Keep the water running into the pan for a couple of minutes to cool the eggs down quickly, then turn it off and let the eggs sit in the cold water for 3–4 minutes.

5 Lift the eggs out of the water, tap each one to crack the shell and peel. Place each egg back in the water to keep it fresh, while you finish peeling the rest.

6 Roughly chop the eggs and place in a bowl. Add the chopped spring onions and dill-pickled cucumber and enough mayonnaise to make a thick, spreadable mixture. Taste and adjust the seasoning accordingly.

7 Butter one side of each slice of bread. Liberally scatter some mustard and cress, watercress or rocket over the butter on two of the slices and pile the filling on top. Cover with more leaves and lightly press the two remaining slices of bread on top. Cut the sandwiches in two with a serrated knife and they are ready to eat.

Nutritional information per portion: Energy 680kcal/2819kJ; Protein 15g; Carbohydrate 30.2g, of which sugars 3.5g; Fat 56.5g, of which saturates 13.6g; Cholesterol 35mg; Calcium 201mg; Fibre 2.3g; Sodium 479mg.

Oatcakes with cheese and pear and walnut chutney

This chutney recipe is ideal for using up hard windfall pears. Its mellow flavour is well suited to a luncheon snack with a selection of strong cheese served with oatcakes.

MAKES ABOUT 1.8KG/4LB

1.2kg/2½lb firm pears
225g/8oz cooking apples
225g/8oz onions
450ml/¾ pint/scant 2 cups cider
    vinegar
175g/6oz/generous 1 cup sultanas
    (golden raisins)
finely grated rind and juice of 1 orange
400g/14oz/2 cups sugar
115g/4oz/1 cup walnuts, roughly
    chopped
2.5ml/½ tsp ground cinnamon
oatcakes
strong blue cheese, such as Roquefort,
    Gorgonzola or Stilton

1 Make the chutney at least 1 month before it is served. Peel and core the fruit, then chop into 2.5cm/1in chunks. Chop the onions into pieces the same size as the fruit chunks. Place in a large preserving pan with the vinegar.

2 Bring to the boil, reduce the heat and simmer for 40 minutes, stirring occasionally. Put the sultanas in a bowl, pour over the orange juice and soak.

3 Add the orange rind, sultanas and orange juice, and the sugar to the pan. Heat gently, stirring continuously, until the sugar has dissolved, then leave to simmer for 30–40 minutes, or until the chutney is thick and no excess liquid remains. Stir frequently to prevent it from sticking.

4 Toast the walnuts over a low heat for 5 minutes, stirring frequently, until lightly coloured. Stir the nuts into the chutney with the ground cinnamon. Spoon the chutney into warmed sterilized jars, cover and seal. Store in a cool, dark place and leave to mature for at least 1 month. Use within 1 year. Serve the chutney with oatcakes and cheese of your choice.

Nutritional information per batch of chutney: Energy 3506kcal/14818kJ; Protein 30.9g; Carbohydrate 705.4g, of which sugars 699.5g; Fat 81.4g, of which saturates 6.4g; Cholesterol 0mg; Calcium 634mg; Fibre 40.7g; Sodium 118mg.

Toasted baguette with salsa

There's something about the mix of chicken and avocado that is very comforting. Mango, too, when combined with oak-smoked chicken and creamy avocado, makes the taste buds tingle.

SERVES 2

2 short baguettes, split lengthways
75g/3oz/6 tbsp butter, melted
2 smoked chicken breasts
300ml/½ pint/1¼ cups natural (plain) yogurt
2.5ml/½ tsp pimentón dulce (smoked Spanish paprika)
60ml/4 tbsp chopped fresh chives
salt and ground black pepper

FOR THE SALSA

2 medium, ripe mangoes
2 ripe Hass avocados
juice of 1 lime
45ml/3 tbsp chopped fresh coriander (cilantro)
5ml/1 tsp mild chilli seasoning

1 To make the salsa cut two mango slices, one from each side of the stone (pit). Peel, chop the flesh and place in a bowl.

2 Halve, remove the stone and peel the avocados, then roughly chop and stir into the mango. Add the lime juice, coriander and chilli seasoning and stir well. Taste and season with salt and black pepper. Leave the salsa for a few hours so that the flavours can develop.

3 Preheat the oven to 200°C/400°F/Gas 6. Pull out some of the inside of each baguette half and brush the halves with melted butter. Place, cut-side uppermost, on a baking tray and bake for about 15 minutes. Remove from the oven, cover with foil and keep warm.

4 Slice the smoked chicken. Generously spoon the salsa into the hollowed baguettes and top with the sliced smoked chicken. Mix the yogurt with the smoked paprika, salt and pepper, and spoon over the chicken. Sprinkle with chopped chives. Eat immediately.

Nutritional information per portion: Energy 1153kcal/4817kJ; Protein 50g; Carbohydrate 79g, of which sugars 36g; Fat 73g, of which saturates 31g; Cholesterol 184mg; Calcium 455mg; Fibre 8.2g; Sodium 1096mg.

French rarebit with sweet shallot and garlic confit

The inspiration for this recipe comes partly from cheese fondue and partly from raclette (melted cheese). If you can imagine grilled fondue on toast, then this is it.

SERVES 4

25g/1oz/2 tbsp butter
5ml/1 tsp Dijon mustard
30ml/2 tbsp medium to sweet white wine
75g/3oz Gruyère or raclette cheese, grated
a pinch of cayenne pepper
2 long thick slices crusty French baguette, cut
   on the slant
2 egg yolks

FOR THE CONFIT

75ml/5 tbsp olive oil
675g/1½lb shallots, quartered
675g/1½lb red onions, finely sliced
4 garlic cloves, thinly sliced (preferably
   smoked garlic)
120ml/4fl oz/½ cup sherry vinegar or half
   dry sherry and half balsamic vinegar
30ml/2 tbsp crème de cassis
salt and ground black pepper

1 To make the confit, heat the oil in a pan over a medium heat. Add the shallots, sliced onions and garlic, stirring to coat with the oil. Add 30ml/2tbsp water and put on the lid. Cook slowly for 20 minutes, without lifting the lid, to steam and soften the onions.

2 Uncover the pan, stir well and continue to cook very slowly for about 1 hour until the onions are very soft and caramelized.

3 Stir the vinegar, or sherry and vinegar, and cassis into the pan and season. Cook the contents for 10 minutes more, to evaporate the vinegar. The confit should now look thick and sticky. Leave to cool, then spoon into a preserving jar, cover with a layer of olive oil and refrigerate.

4 Preheat the grill (broiler). Put the butter, mustard, white wine, cheese and cayenne pepper in a small pan and slowly melt over a gentle heat. Set aside for a moment.

5 Toast the slices of baguette on one side. Beat the egg yolks into the melted cheese and spread over the un-toasted side of the bread. Put under the grill for 2–3 minutes until browned and bubbling. Serve with a good dollop of the sweet onion and garlic confit.

Nutritional information per portion: Energy 513kcal/2132kJ; Protein 12g; Carbohydrate 38g, of which sugars 13g; Fat 34g, of which saturates 11g; Cholesterol 133mg; Calcium 281mg; Fibre 4.4g; Sodium 541mg.

Potato skins with Cajun dip

Divinely crisp and naughty, these potato skins are really simple to make. They are great on their own or served with this piquant dip as a garnish or on the side.

SERVES 4

2 large baking potatoes
vegetable oil, for deep-frying

FOR THE DIP
120ml/4fl oz/$1/2$ cup natural
   (plain) yogurt
1 garlic clove, crushed
5ml/1 tsp tomato purée (paste) or
   2.5ml/$1/2$ tsp green chilli purée or
   $1/2$ small green chilli, chopped
1.5ml/$1/4$ tsp celery salt
salt and ground black pepper

1 Preheat the oven to 180°C/350°F/Gas 4. Bake the potatoes for 45–50 minutes until they are tender.

2 Cut the potatoes in half and then scoop out the flesh, leaving a thin layer on the skins. Keep the flesh for another meal. Cut the potatoes in half once more.

3 To make the dip, mix together all the ingredients and chill.

4 Heat a 1cm/$1/2$in layer of oil in a pan or deep-fryer. Fry the potatoes until they are crisp and golden. Drain on kitchen paper, then sprinkle with salt and black pepper. Serve the potato skins with a bowl of dip or a dollop of dip in each skin.

Nutritional information per portion: Energy 210kcal/871kJ; Protein 2.7g; Carbohydrate 12.5g, of which sugars 3.3g; Fat 17g, of which saturates 2.2g; Cholesterol 0mg; Calcium 61mg; Fibre 0.7g; Sodium 35mg.

Garlic mushrooms and walnut and goat's cheese on bruschetta

Bruschetta is a simple and satisfying snack. It can be topped with just about anything you fancy. Here we show two options: garlic mushrooms and walnuts with creamy goat's cheese.

SERVES 4

4 large slices of sourdough bread
75g/3oz/6 tbsp butter, and extra to spread

FOR THE MUSHROOM TOPPING

3 shallots, finely chopped
2 garlic cloves, finely chopped
675g/1½lb field (portabello) or
**   chestnut mushrooms, thickly sliced**
75ml/5 tbsp dry white wine
45ml/3 tbsp chopped fresh parsley
salt and ground black pepper

FOR THE CHEESE TOPPING

200g/7oz chèvre or other semi-soft
**   goat's cheese**
50g/2oz/½ cup walnut pieces
120ml/4fl oz/½ cup French dressing

1 Toast the bread on both sides on a hot ridged griddle to give the bread a striped charred effect. The ridged griddle must be heated until very hot. If you don't have a griddle, toast under a hot grill (broiler) on both sides until quite dark. Brush the toasted bread with the extra melted butter and keep warm.

2 For for the mushroom topping, melt the butter in a frying pan, add the shallots and garlic, and cook for 5 minutes until golden. Add the mushrooms and toss well. Fry over a high heat for 1 minute. Pour over the wine and season well. Keep the heat high and cook until the wine evaporates. Lightly stir in the parsley. Pile the mushrooms on to the bruschetta and serve.

3 Cut the goat's cheese into twelve slices and place three on each piece of bread. Grill (broil) for 3 minutes, until the cheese is melting and beginning to brown. Sprinkle with the walnuts and drizzle with the French dressing.

Nutritional information per portion (mushroom topping): Energy 297kcal/1240kJ; Protein 8.1g; Carbohydrate 25.9g, of which sugars 2.9g; Fat 17.3g, of which saturates 10.2g; Cholesterol 40mg; Calcium 107mg; Fibre 3.3g; Sodium 420mg.
Nutritional information per portion (cheese topping): Energy 520kcal/2159kJ; Protein 16g; Carbohydrate 26g, of which sugars 7g; Fat 42g, of which saturates 13g; Cholesterol 47mg; Calcium 113mg; Fibre 0.6g; Sodium 500mg.

Garlic and herb bread

This irresistible garlic bread includes plenty of fresh mixed herbs. You can vary the overall flavour according to the combination of herbs you choose.

SERVES 3–4

1 baguette or bloomer loaf

FOR THE GARLIC AND HERB BUTTER

115g/4oz/½ cup unsalted butter, softened

5–6 large garlic cloves, finely chopped or crushed

30–45ml/2–3 tbsp chopped mixed fresh herbs (such as parsley, chervil and a little tarragon)

15ml/1 tbsp chopped fresh chives

coarse salt and ground black pepper

1 Preheat the oven to 200°C/400°F/Gas 6. Make the garlic and herb butter by beating the butter with the garlic, mixed herbs, chives and seasoning.

2 Cut the bread into 1cm/½in thick diagonal slices, but be sure to leave them attached at the base so that the loaf itself stays intact.

3 Spread the garlic and herb butter between the slices evenly, being careful not to detach them, and then spread any remaining butter over the top of the loaf.

4 Wrap the loaf in foil and bake in the preheated oven for 20–25 minutes, until the butter is melted and the crust is golden and crisp. Cut the loaf into slices to serve.

Nutritional information per portion: Energy 920kcal/3877kJ; Protein 22.1g; Carbohydrate 135.1g, of which sugars 7.2g; Fat 36.2g, of which saturates 20.8g; Cholesterol 82mg; Calcium 317mg; Fibre 6.3g; Sodium 1714mg.

Hummus

This Middle Eastern dish is made from cooked chickpeas, ground to a paste and flavoured with garlic, lemon juice, tahini, olive oil and cumin. Serve with toasted pitta bread or crudités.

SERVES 4–6

400g/14oz can chickpeas, drained
60ml/4 tbsp tahini
2–3 garlic cloves, chopped
juice of 1/2–1 lemon
a sprinkling of cayenne pepper
small pinch to 1.5ml/1/4 tsp ground
   cumin, or more to taste
salt and ground black pepper

1 Using a potato masher or food processor, coarsely mash the chickpeas. If you prefer a smoother purée, process them in a food processor or blender until smooth.

2 Mix the tahini into the chickpeas, then stir in the garlic, lemon juice, cayenne, cumin and salt and pepper to taste. If needed, add a little water. Serve at room temperature.

Nutritional information per portion: Energy 140kcal/586kJ; Protein 6.9g; Carbohydrate 11.2g, of which sugars 0.4g; Fat 7.8g, of which saturates 1.1g; Cholesterol 0mg; Calcium 97mg; Fibre 3.6g; Sodium 149mg.

Steak sandwich with basil aioli and caramelized onions

In this delightful lunchtime treat, thick-cut sirloin steak is marinated and chargrilled, then sliced thinly and piled on to a toasted ciabatta loaf that has been generously spread with a rich basil and garlic aioli. To top it off, a heap of caramelized onions. Irresistible.

SERVES 4

400g/14oz beef sirloin, cut as one piece
30ml/2 tbsp teriyaki marinade
5ml/1 tsp sesame oil
black olive or sun-dried tomato ciabatta
  loaves, split in half
olive oil, for brushing
75g/3oz bag fresh salad leaves

FOR THE BASIL AIOLI
175ml/6fl oz/³/₄ cup light olive oil
115g/4oz/2 cups fresh basil leaves

2 large garlic cloves, crushed
1 egg yolk
fresh lemon juice
salt and ground black pepper

FOR THE CARAMELIZED ONIONS
50g/2oz/¹/₄ cup unsalted butter
2 large onions, finely sliced
10ml/2 tsp caster (superfine) sugar
15ml/1 tbsp balsamic vinegar

1 Trim any fat or sinew from the beef and place the beef in a glass dish. Liberally spoon the marinade and oil over the meat. Cover and leave to marinate overnight or for at least 4 hours in the refrigerator, turning occasionally.

2 Make the aioli up to 2 hours before serving. Put the olive oil and basil in a blender or food processor and process until smooth. Pour into a jug (pitcher). Process together the garlic, egg yolk and a pinch of salt. With the motor running, pour in half the basil oil, in a thin steady stream, until the mixture starts to thicken. Stop the machine and scrape down the sides. Add a squeeze of lemon juice, start the machine again, and pour in the oil until the aioli is quite thick. Put it in the refrigerator until needed.

3 Caramelize the onions. Melt the butter in a pan. Add the onions and stir to coat well. Add 30ml/2 tbsp water, cover and cook over a gentle heat for 10 minutes. Uncover, sprinkle with the sugar and vinegar and turn up the heat. Cook for 10 minutes more, stirring from time to time. Set aside.

4 Heat a ridged griddle pan until smoking hot. Remove the meat from the marinade and pat dry with kitchen paper. Sear the meat on the griddle for 2–3 minutes on each side, then reduce the heat to medium and cook the meat, without moving, for another 4 minutes.

5 Turn the meat over and cook for 4 minutes more. Lift on to a plate, cover with foil and leave for 10 minutes to allow the meat to relax. This cooking time produces medium rare meat, but if you like your meat well done, cook for a little longer.

6 Split the ciabatta loaves and brush with olive oil, then toast on the griddle or under the grill (broiler). Wrap in foil to keep warm while you slice the beef thinly.

7 Spread one half of the bread liberally with the basil aioli, top with the beef, then the onions, more aioli and finally the ciabatta top. Cut the sandwich in two or four and eat immediately, accompanied by the salad leaves.

Nutritional information per portion: Energy 1036kcal/4320kJ; Protein 37g; Carbohydrate 63g, of which sugars 11g; Fat 72g, of which saturates 17g; Cholesterol 130mg; Calcium 234mg; Fibre 1.2g; Sodium 971mg.

Prawn and dill tartlets and chicken and asparagus tartlets

Use these fillings with prepared, pre-baked tartlet shells if you can find them, or alternatively make the delicious buttery shortcrust pastry below. Both of these tartlets are scrumptious and the small packages make them totally moreish.

MAKES 18

200g/7oz/1³/₄ cups plain (all-purpose) flour
125g/4¹/₂ oz/9 tbsp butter, softened
150ml/¹/₄ pint/²/₃ cup cold water
salad leaves, to serve

FOR THE PRAWN (SHRIMP) FILLING:
45g/1¹/₂oz/scant ¹/₄ cup butter
20g/³/₄oz/¹/₄ cup plain (all-purpose) flour
475ml/16fl oz/2 cups single (light) cream
275g/10oz cooked prawns (shrimp)
salt and ground white pepper
25ml/1¹/₂ tbsp chopped fresh dill sprigs

FOR THE CHICKEN AND ASPARAGUS FILLING:
65g/2¹/₂oz/5 tbsp butter
225g/8oz fresh asparagus, cut into 2cm/³/₄in pieces
15ml/1 tbsp vegetable oil
225g/8oz skinless, boneless chicken breasts, cut into 2cm/³/₄in cubes
20g/³/₄oz/¹/₄ cup plain (all-purpose) flour
475ml/16fl oz/2 cups single (light) cream
salt and ground white pepper
45ml/3 tbsp chopped fresh parsley, to garnish

1 Preheat the oven to 200°C/400°F/Gas 6. Sift the flour into a large bowl. Cut the butter into small pieces, add to the flour and rub in until the mixture resembles fine breadcrumbs. Add the water, or enough to form a dough.

2 On a lightly floured surface, roll out the pastry and cut circles to fit 7cm/2³/₄in diameter fluted tart tins.

3 Cut a 13cm/5in square of foil to line each pastry shell and fill with a handful of dried beans. Chill for 30 minutes to rest the pastry, then bake for 10–15 minutes until golden. Remove the beans and foil for the last 5 minutes.

4 To make the prawn filling, melt the butter in a pan over a medium heat, and stir in the flour. Cook for 3–5 minutes until pale beige. Stir in the cream and cook, stirring, for about 5 minutes, until thickened. Stir the prawns into the sauce and heat gently for 3–4 minutes. Season well.

5 To make the chicken and asparagus filling, melt 25g/1oz/2 tbsp of the butter in a frying pan over a medium heat. Add the asparagus, toss to coat with butter and cook, stirring, for about 4 minutes, until tender. Remove and set aside on a plate.

6 In the same pan, heat the cooking oil over a medium heat. Add the chicken and cook for about 5 minutes, stirring, until it is no longer pink. Set aside.

7 Melt the remaining butter in a separate pan over a medium heat and stir in the flour. Cook the roux for 3–5 minutes until pale beige-coloured. Slowly stir in the cream and cook, stirring constantly, for about 5 minutes until the sauce has thickened. Add the asparagus and chicken and heat for 3–4 minutes. Season well.

8 Fill half the tart cases with the creamed prawns, and sprinkle with fresh dill. Fill the rest with the chicken and asparagus, and sprinkle with fresh parsley. Serve with salad leaves.

Nutritional information per portion (one of each tartlet): Energy 274kcal/1138kJ; Protein 9g; Carbohydrate 11g, of which sugars 1.7g; Fat 21.9g, of which saturates 13.4g; Cholesterol 95mg; Calcium 83mg; Fibre 0.6g; Sodium 131mg.

Smoked mozzarella and ham pizza with rocket

This home-made pizza is a delight – gooey smoked cheese and ham on a bed of onions, dripping off a thin and crispy base. The rocket is thrown on top to wilt into the cheese.

MAKES 2 PIZZAS

75ml/5 tbsp olive oil
1kg/2¼lb onions, finely sliced
15ml/1 tbsp chopped fresh rosemary
10ml/2 tsp dried oregano
115g/4oz smoked ham, sliced and torn
1 smoked mozzarella, peeled and sliced
30ml/2 tbsp grated Parmesan cheese
100g/4oz rocket (arugula)
salt and ground black pepper

FOR THE PIZZA DOUGH

25g/1oz fresh yeast, 15g/½oz dried
    active baking yeast or 2 sachets easy-
    blend (rapid-rise) dried yeast
a pinch of sugar
350g/12oz/3 cups Italian "00" flour, plus
    extra for dusting
30ml/2 tbsp olive oil, plus extra for drizzling
5ml/1 tsp salt

1 If using fresh yeast, cream it with the sugar in a bowl and whisk in 250ml/8fl oz/1 cup warm water. Leave for 10 minutes until frothy.

2 Sift the flour into a bowl, pour in the yeast, oil and salt, mix with a round-bladed knife, then form a soft dough. Knead for 10 minutes until smooth and elastic. Place in a clean, oiled bowl, cover with a damp towel and leave for 1 hour until doubled.

3 Heat the oil and add the onions. Cook over a gentle heat for 20 minutes. Stir in the herbs and season.

4 Preheat the oven to 240°C/475°F/ Gas 9. Knock back (punch down) the pizza dough. Divide the dough in half and roll out to make two rounds 25–30cm/10–12in in diameter, and about 5mm/¼in thick. Slide these on to two floured, flat baking sheets.

5 Cover the pizza bases with the onions. Sprinkle over the ham and lay the mozzarella on top. Sprinkle with the cheese.

6 Bake in the oven for about 15 minutes until golden and crisp. Pile the rocket on top and serve.

Nutritional information per pizza: Energy 1159kcal/6225kJ; Protein 58g; Carbohydrate 176g, of which sugars 34g; Fat 74g, of which saturates 17g; Cholesterol 31mg; Calcium 678mg; Fibre 17.1g; Sodium 2589mg.

Tomato and tapenade tarts

These tempting individual tarts look and taste fantastic, and demand very little time or effort. The mascarpone cheese topping melts as it cooks to make a smooth, creamy sauce.

SERVES 4

vegetable oil, for greasing
500g/1¼ lb puff pastry, thawed if frozen
plain (all-purpose) flour, for dusting
60ml/4 tbsp green olive tapenade
500g/1¼ lb cherry tomatoes
**90g/3½oz/scant ½ cup mascarpone
   cheese**
salt and ground black peper

1 Preheat the oven to 220°C/ 425°F/Gas 7. Lightly grease a large baking sheet and sprinkle it with water. Roll out the pastry on a lightly floured surface and cut out four 16cm/6½in rounds, using a bowl or small plate as a guide.

2 Transfer the pastry rounds to the prepared baking sheet. Using the tip of a sharp knife, mark a shallow cut 1cm/½in in from the edge of each round to form a rim.

3 Spread half the tapenade over the pastry rounds, keeping it inside the marked rim. Cut half the tomatoes in half. Pile all of the tomatoes on the pastry, keeping them inside the rim. Season lightly.

4 Bake for 20 minutes. Dot with the remaining tapenade. Spoon a little mascarpone on the centre of the tomatoes and season. Bake for a further 10 minutes, until the mascarpone has melted. Serve warm.

Nutritional information per portion: Energy 543kcal/2269kJ; Protein 10.2g; Carbohydrate 50.8g, of which sugars 6.2g; Fat 35.9g, of which saturates 2.4g; Cholesterol 9mg; Calcium 91mg; Fibre 1.7g; Sodium 736mg.

Cheese and onion flan

Baking savoury tarts is just as satisfying as making buns and cakes. Made with yeast dough, this French classic is great for kneading out tensions and troubles.

SERVES 4

15g/¹⁄₂oz/1 tbsp butter
1 onion, halved and sliced
2 eggs
250ml/8fl oz/1 cup single (light) cream
225g/8oz strong semi-soft cheese, rind
    removed (about 175g/6oz without rind),
    sliced
salt and ground black pepper
salad leaves, to serve

FOR THE YEAST DOUGH

10ml/2 tsp dried yeast
120ml/4fl oz/¹⁄₂ cup full cream (whole) milk
5ml/1 tsp sugar
1 egg yolk
225g/8oz/2 cups plain (all-purpose) flour
2.5ml/¹⁄₂ tsp salt
50g/2oz/4 tbsp butter, softened

1 To make the dough, place the yeast in a bowl. Warm the milk in a small pan until it is at body temperature and stir into the yeast with the sugar. Continue stirring until the yeast has dissolved completely. Leave the yeast mixture to stand for about 3 minutes, then beat in the egg yolk.

2 Put the flour and salt in a food processor or blender fitted with a metal blade, and pulse to combine. With the machine running, slowly pour in the yeast mixture. Scrape down the sides and continue processing for 2–3 minutes. Add the softened butter and process for another 30 seconds.

3 Transfer the dough to a lightly greased bowl. Cover with a dish towel and allow to rise in a warm place for 1 hour until the dough has doubled in bulk.

4 Remove the dough from the bowl and place on a lightly floured surface. Knock back (punch down) the dough. Sprinkle a little more flour on the work surface and roll out the dough to a 30cm/12in round.

5 Line a 23cm/9in flan tin (quiche pan) or dish with the dough. Gently press it into the tin or dish and trim off any overhanging pieces, leaving a 3mm/¹⁄₈in rim around the flan case. Cover with a dish towel, set aside in a warm place and leave the dough to rise for 30 minutes, or until puffy.

6 Meanwhile, melt the butter in a heavy pan and add the onion. Cover the pan and cook over a medium-low heat for about 15 minutes, until softened, stirring occasionally. Remove the lid and continue cooking, stirring frequently, until the onion is very soft and caramelized.

7 Preheat the oven to 180°C/350°F/Gas 4. Beat the eggs and cream. Season and stir in the onion.

8 Arrange the cheese on the base of the flan case. Pour over the egg mixture and bake for 30–35 minutes until the base is golden and the centre is just set. Cool slightly on a wire rack and serve warm with salad leaves.

COOK'S TIP
If you prefer to use easy-blend (rapid-rise) dried yeast, omit step 1. Beat the egg yolk and milk together in a jug (pitcher). Add the dry yeast to the flour and salt in the food processor or blender, and pulse to combine. Pour in the egg and milk mixture, and proceed with the recipe as normal.

Nutritional information per portion: Energy 717kcal/2990kJ; Protein 24.8g; Carbohydrate 50.6g, of which sugars 6.9g; Fat 46.5g, of which saturates 28.1g; Cholesterol 288mg; Calcium 350mg; Fibre 2.3g; Sodium 735mg.

Coffee and Teatime Treats

Home-made snacks are guaranteed to lift your spirits between meals. Here are a variety of taste experiences – chewy, chocolately, crunchy, creamy or oozing with jam or custard. Try Sugar-crusted Shortbread Rounds or Baklava with a morning coffee, and Coffee and Walnut Swiss Roll or Black Forest Gateau for teatime. The physical preparation – kneading, rolling, spooning, shredding chocolate and sprinkling sugar – adds to the enjoyment, along with the sweet aroma of baking.

Sugar-crusted shortbread rounds

Shortbread should always be in the biscuit tin or cookie jar. A good shortbread should melt in the mouth, taste buttery but never greasy, and always make you crave for more.

MAKES ABOUT 24

450g/1lb/2 cups salted butter
225g/8oz/1 heaped cup caster (superfine) sugar
450g/1lb/4 cups plain (all-purpose) flour

225g/8oz/scant 1½ cups ground rice or rice flour
5ml/1 tsp salt
demerara (raw) sugar, to decorate
golden caster (superfine) sugar, for dusting

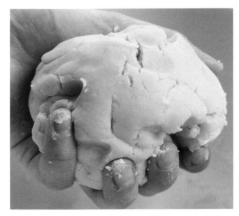

1 Make sure all the ingredients are at room temperature. Salted butter has more flavour than unsalted, but if you only have unsalted, then it's fine to use it. In a food processor (blender) or bowl, cream the butter and sugar together until light, pale and fluffy. If you used a food processor, scrape the mixture out into a mixing bowl.

2 Sift together the flour, ground rice or rice flour and salt and stir into the butter and sugar with a wooden spoon, until the mixture resembles fine breadcrumbs. (The rice flour adds a toothsome grittiness and shortness to the dough.)

3 Working quickly, gather the dough together with your hand, then put it on a clean work surface. Knead lightly together until it forms a ball but take care not to over-knead or the shortbread will be tough and greasy. Lightly roll into a sausage shape, about 7.5cm/3in thick. Wrap in clear film (plastic wrap) and chill until firm. Preheat the oven to 190°C/375°F/Gas 5.

4 Pour the demerara sugar on to a sheet of baking parchment. Unwrap the dough and roll in the sugar until evenly coated. Using a large, sharp knife, slice the roll into discs about 1cm/½in thick.

5 Place the discs on to two baking sheets lined with baking parchment, spacing well apart. Bake for 20–25 minutes until set and pale gold, not brown.

6 Remove from the oven and sprinkle with golden caster sugar. Allow to cool on the baking sheet for 10 minutes before transferring to a wire rack to cool completely.

Nutritional information per biscuit: Energy 275kcal/1147kJ; Protein 2.5g; Carbohydrate 32g, of which sugars 10.2g; Fat 15.7g, of which saturates 9.8g; Cholesterol 40mg; Calcium 37mg; Fibre 0.8g; Sodium 197mg.

Soda scones with jam

Buttered scones with jam are the ultimate teatime treat. The contrast of warm, buttery scone, home-made jam bursting with fruit, and thick clotted cream creates a delightful series of textures, and a perfect edible accompaniment to a conversation with friends.

MAKES ABOUT 12

450g/1lb/4 cups self-raising (self-rising) flour or 450g/1lb/4 cups plain (all-purpose) flour and 10ml/2 tsp baking powder
5ml/1 tsp salt
50g/2oz/¼ cup butter, chilled and cut into cubes

15ml/1 tbsp lemon juice
about 400ml/14fl oz/1²/₃ cups full cream (whole) milk, plus extra to glaze
fruit jam and clotted cream, or double (heavy) cream, to serve

1 Preheat the oven to 230°C/450°F/Gas 8. Sift the flour, salt and baking powder, if using, into a mixing bowl. Rub in the butter until the mixture resembles fine breadcrumbs.

2 Whisk the lemon juice into the milk and leave for about 1 minute to thicken slightly, then pour into the flour mixture and mix quickly to form a soft but manageable dough. The wetter the mixture the lighter the resulting scone will be, but if too wet they will spread out while baking in the oven.

3 Knead the dough lightly to form a ball, then roll it out on a floured surface to a thickness of at least 2.5cm/1in. Using a 5cm/2in biscuit cutter and dipping it into flour each time, stamp out 12 scones, and place them on a well-floured baking sheet. Re-roll any trimmings and cut out more if you can.

4 Brush the tops of the scones lightly with a little milk and then bake them for about 20 minutes, or until risen and golden brown. Remove the tray from the oven and wrap the scones in a clean dish towel to keep them warm and soft until ready to serve. Eat with your favourite fruit jam and a generous dollop of cream.

Nutritional information per scone: Energy 170kcal/720kJ; Protein 4.5g; Carbohydrate 29.9g, of which sugars 2.1g; Fat 4.4g, of which saturates 2.6g; Cholesterol 11mg; Calcium 172mg; Fibre 1.2g; Sodium 338mg.

Fruity breakfast bars

This delightfully quick method gives satisfyingly crunchy and chewy results. Use them for breakfast on the go or as an accompaniment to your first coffee of the day.

MAKES 12

270g/10oz jar apple sauce
115g/4oz/¹/₂ cup ready-to-eat dried apricots, chopped
115g/4oz/³/₄ cup raisins
50g/2oz/¹/₄ cup demerara (raw) sugar
50g/2oz/¹/₃ cup sunflower seeds
25g/1oz/2 tbsp sesame seeds
25g/1oz/¹/₄ cup pumpkin seeds
75g/3oz/scant 1 cup rolled oats
75g/3oz/²/₃ cup self-raising (self-rising) wholemeal (whole-wheat) flour
50g/2oz/²/₃ cup desiccated (dry unsweetened shredded) coconut
2 eggs

1 Preheat the oven to 200°C/400°F/Gas 6. Grease a 20cm/8in square shallow baking tin (pan) and line with baking parchment.

2 Put the apple sauce in a large bowl with the apricots, raisins, sugar and the sunflower, sesame and pumpkin seeds and stir together with a wooden spoon until thoroughly mixed.

3 Add the oats, flour, coconut and eggs to the fruit mixture and gently stir together until evenly combined.

4 Turn the mixture into the tin and spread to the edges in an even layer. Bake for about 25 minutes or until golden and just firm to the touch.

5 Leave to cool in the tin, then lift out on to a board and cut into bars.

Nutritional information per bar: Energy 207kcal/871kJ; Protein 4.9g; Carbohydrate 29.3g, of which sugars 19.2g; Fat 8.7g, of which saturates 3g; Cholesterol 32mg; Calcium 65mg; Fibre 2.8g; Sodium 24mg.

Chocolate and prune refrigerator bars

Wickedly self-indulgent and very easy to make, these fruity chocolate bars will keep for 2–3 days in the refrigerator – if they don't all get eaten as soon as they are ready.

MAKES 12

250g/9oz milk chocolate
115g/4oz digestive biscuits (graham crackers)
115g/4oz/¹/₂ cup ready-to-eat prunes
50g/2oz/¹/₄ cup unsalted butter

1 Break the chocolate into small pieces and place in a heatproof bowl.

2 Add the butter and melt in the microwave on high for 1–2 minutes. Stir to mix and set aside. (Alternatively, place the bowl over a pan of gently simmering water and leave until melted, stirring the mixture frequently.)

3 Put the biscuits in a plastic bag and seal, then bash into small pieces with a rolling pin. Roughly chop the prunes and stir into the melted chocolate with the biscuits.

4 Spoon the mixture into a 20cm/8in square cake pan (tin) and chill for 1–2 hours until set. Remove from the refrigerator and, with a sharp knife, cut into 12 bars and serve.

Nutritional information per bar: Energy 197kcal/826kJ; Protein 2.5g; Carbohydrate 21.7g, of which sugars 16.4g; Fat 11.8g, of which saturates 6.8g; Cholesterol 18mg; Calcium 59mg; Fibre 0.9g; Sodium 102mg.

Chocolate brownies

This classic American recipe is popular with lovers of all things sweet and chocolatey. The double dose of chocolate makes them rich and intense.

MAKES 15

75g/3oz dark (bittersweet) chocolate

115g/4oz/½ cup butter, plus extra for greasing

4 eggs, beaten

10ml/2 tsp vanilla extract

400g/14oz/2 cups caster (superfine) sugar

115g/4oz/1 cup plain (all-purpose) flour

25g/1oz/¼ cup unsweetened cocoa powder

115g/4oz dark (bittersweet) chocolate chips

115g/4oz/1 cup chopped walnuts

1 Preheat the oven to 190°C/375°F/ Gas 5. Grease an 18 x 28cm/7 x 11in shallow baking tin (pan) and line with baking parchment.

2 Break the dark chocolate into pieces and put it in a heatproof bowl with the butter. Place the bowl over a pan of barely simmering water and leave the chocolate and butter to melt. Remove from the heat and stir in the beaten eggs, vanilla and sugar. Mix together well.

3 Sift the flour with the cocoa powder into the chocolate mixture. Gently stir in with the chocolate chips and walnuts. Pour the mixture into the tin and level the surface.

4 Put the tin in the oven and bake for about 35 minutes. To test if the brownies are fully cooked, gently shake the tin. The cake should be set but moist. Leave to cool in the tin. Cut into squares when cold.

Nutritional information per brownie: Energy 285kcal/1190kJ; Protein 3.1g; Carbohydrate 29.6g, of which sugars 25.9g; Fat 18g, of which saturates 10.7g; Cholesterol 61mg; Calcium 37mg; Fibre 0.9g; Sodium 98mg.

White chocolate brownies

These irresistible brownies are packed full of creamy white chocolate and lots of juicy dried fruit. They are best served cut into very small bitesize portions as they are incredibly rich.

MAKES 18

75g/3oz/6 tbsp unsalted butter, diced
400g/14oz white chocolate, chopped
3 eggs
90g/3¹/₂oz/¹/₂ cup golden caster (superfine) sugar
10ml/2 tsp vanilla extract
90g/3¹/₂oz/³/₄ cup sultanas (golden raisins)
coarsely grated rind of 1 lemon, plus 15ml/1 tbsp juice
200g/7oz/1³/₄ cups plain (all-purpose) flour

1 Preheat the oven to 190°C/ 375°F/Gas 5. Grease and line a 28 x 20cm/11 x 8in shallow baking tin (pan) with baking parchment.

2 Put the butter and 300g/11oz of the chocolate in a heatproof bowl and melt over a pan of simmering water. Remove from the heat.

3 Beat in the eggs and sugar. Add the vanilla, sultanas, rind and juice, flour and the remaining chocolate.

4 Turn the mixture into the prepared tin and spread the mixture right into the corners.

5 Bake for about 20 minutes, or until slightly risen and the surface is only just turning golden. The centre should still be slightly soft.

6 Leave to cool in the tin. Using a sharp knife, cut the brownies into small squares and remove from the tin before serving.

Nutritional information per cookie: Energy 232kcal/973kJ; Protein 4g; Carbohydrate 30.3g, of which sugars 21.8g; Fat 11.4g, of which saturates 6.5g; Cholesterol 41mg; Calcium 86mg; Fibre 0.4g; Sodium 65mg.

Giant triple chocolate cookies

Here is the ultimate cookie, packed with chocolate and macadamia nuts. You will have to be patient when they come out of the oven, as they are too soft to move until completely cold!

MAKES 12

90g/3½oz milk chocolate

90g/3½oz white chocolate

300g/11oz dark (bittersweet) chocolate (minimum 70 per cent cocoa solids)

90g/3½oz/7 tbsp unsalted butter, at room temperature, diced

5ml/1 tsp vanilla extract

150g/5oz/¾ cup light muscovado (brown) sugar

150g/5oz/1¼ cups self-raising (self-rising) flour

100g/3½oz/scant 1 cup macadamia nut halves

1 Preheat the oven to 180°C/350°F/Gas 4. Line two baking sheets with baking parchment. Coarsely chop the milk and white chocolate and put them in a bowl. Chop 200g/7oz of the dark chocolate into very large chunks, at least 2cm/¾in in size. Set aside.

2 Break up the remaining dark chocolate and place in a heatproof bowl set over a pan of barely simmering water. Stir until melted and smooth. Remove from the heat and stir in the butter, then the vanilla extract and muscovado sugar.

3 Add the flour and mix gently. Add half the dark chocolate chunks, all the milk and white chocolate and the nuts and fold together.

4 Spoon 12 mounds on to the baking sheets. Press the remaining dark chocolate chunks into the top of each cookie. Bake for about 12 minutes until just beginning to colour. Cool on the baking sheets.

Nutritional information per cookie: Energy 413kcal/1727kJ; Protein 3.9g; Carbohydrate 48.4g, of which sugars 38.6g; Fat 24g, of which saturates 11.6g; Cholesterol 18mg; Calcium 69mg; Fibre 1.8g; Sodium 117mg.

Buñuelos

These lovely little puffs look like miniature doughnuts and taste so good it is hard not to over-indulge. Serve them with coffee as a special treat when friends drop in.

MAKES 12

225g/8oz/2 cups plain (all-purpose) flour
a pinch of salt
5ml/1 tsp baking powder
2.5ml/½ tsp ground anise
115g/4oz/generous ½ cup caster
  (superfine) sugar
1 large (US extra large) egg
120ml/4fl oz/½ cup full cream
  (whole) milk
50g/2oz/¼ cup butter
vegetable oil, for deep-frying
10ml/2 tsp ground cinnamon
cinnamon sticks, to decorate

1 Sift the flour, salt, baking powder and ground anise into a mixing bowl. Add 30ml/2 tbsp of the caster sugar. Whisk the egg and milk. Melt the butter in a pan. Pour the egg and milk mixture gradually into the flour, stirring, until well blended, then add the butter. Mix to make a soft dough.

2 Knead the dough on a lightly floured surface for about 10 minutes, until smooth. Divide into 12 pieces and roll into balls. Flatten each ball with your hand and make a hole in the centre with the floured handle of a wooden spoon.

3 Heat the oil to 190°C/375°F, or until a cube of dried bread floats and turns a golden colour in 30–60 seconds. Fry the *buñuelos* in batches, turning them during cooking. When they are puffy and golden, lift them out using a slotted spoon and lay them on a double layer of kitchen paper to drain.

4 Mix the remaining caster sugar with the ground cinnamon in a bowl. Toss the *buñuelos* in the mixture until lightly coated and either serve at once or leave to cool. Decorate with cinnamon sticks.

Nutritional information per bun: Energy 169kcal/715kJ; Protein 4g; Carbohydrate 34.1g, of which sugars 8.7g; Fat 2.8g, of which saturates 1.4g; Cholesterol 21mg; Calcium 63mg; Fibre 1g; Sodium 24mg.

Butterscotch nut muffins

Lining a muffin tin with paper cases avoids the frustration of struggling with muffins that insist on sticking to the tin. Make up the two mixtures the night before and stir them together first thing next day for an irresistible mid-morning treat. Instead of butterscotch, try adding chocolate chips, marshmallows or blueberries.

MAKES 9–12

150g/5oz butterscotch sweets (candies)
225g/8oz/2 cups plain (all-purpose) flour
90g/3¹/₂ oz/7 tbsp golden caster (superfine) sugar
10ml/2 tsp baking powder
2.5ml/¹/₂ tsp salt

1 large (US extra large) egg, beaten
150ml/¹/₄ pint/²/₃ cup full cream (whole) milk
50ml/2fl oz/¹/₄ cup sunflower oil or melted butter
75g/3oz/³/₄ cup chopped hazelnuts
butter for greasing, if needed

1 Preheat the oven to 200°C/400°F/Gas 6. Line a 9–12 cup muffin tin (pan) with paper cases or grease with butter. With floured fingers, break the butterscotch sweets into small chunks. Toss them in a little flour, if necessary, to prevent them from sticking together.

2 Sift together the flour, sugar, baking powder and salt into a mixing bowl. Whisk together the egg, milk and oil or melted butter, then stir the mixture into the dry ingredients with the sweets and nuts. Only lightly stir together as there should still be a few lumps of flour in the mixture.

3 Spoon the mixture evenly into the prepared muffin tin, filling the paper cases about half full. Bake for 20 minutes until well risen and golden brown. Cool in the tin for 5 minutes, then remove and transfer the muffins to a cooling rack. Serve slightly warm, or cold, on the day they are made.

COOK'S TIP

For an extra luxurious touch, try spreading these with a treat called dulce de leche; it is rather like condensed milk that has been boiled until caramelized. Just drizzle this over the muffins before eating.

Nutritional information per muffin: Energy 224kcal/941kJ; Protein 3.9g; Carbohydrate 31.7g, of which sugars 14.6g; Fat 10g, of which saturates 2.1g; Cholesterol 19mg; Calcium 66mg; Fibre 1g; Sodium 55mg.

Chocolate butterscotch and hazelnut bars

Unashamedly rich and sweet, these bars are perfect for chocoholics of all ages. Make sure the chocolate topping is set before cutting into bars.

MAKES 24

225g/8oz/2 cups plain (all-purpose) flour
2.5ml/¹/₂ tsp baking powder
115g/4oz/¹/₂ cup unsalted butter
50g/2oz/¹/₃ cup light muscovado (brown) sugar
150g/5oz plain (semisweet) chocolate
30ml/2 tbsp ground almonds

FOR THE TOPPING

175g/6oz/³/₄ cup unsalted butter
115g/4oz/¹/₂ cup caster (superfine) sugar
30ml/2 tbsp golden (light corn) syrup
175ml/6fl oz/³/₄ cup sweetened condensed milk
150g/5oz/1¹/₄ cups whole toasted hazelnuts
225g/8oz plain (semisweet) chocolate, broken into squares

1 Preheat the oven to 160°C/325°F/Gas 3. Lightly grease a shallow 30 x 20cm/12 x 8in tin (pan). Sift the flour and baking powder into a large bowl.

2 Rub in the butter until the mixture resembles coarse breadcrumbs and stir in the sugar. Melt the chocolate in a heatproof bowl over simmering water, add to the mixture with the almonds and mix to a smooth dough.

3 Press the dough into the tin, prick with a fork and bake for 25–30 minutes until firm. Leave to cool in the tin.

4 For the topping, place the butter, sugar, golden syrup and condensed milk in a pan. Heat gently, stirring, until the butter has melted and the sugar dissolved. Simmer, stirring, until golden, then stir in the hazelnuts. Pour over the cooled cooked base and leave to set.

5 Melt the chocolate in a heatproof bowl over barely simmering water. Spread the melted chocolate over the butterscotch layer, then leave to set before cutting into bars to serve.

Nutritional information per bar: Energy 305kcal/1273kJ; Protein 3.5g; Carbohydrate 30g, of which sugars 22.5g; Fat 19.8g, of which saturates 9.7g; Cholesterol 29mg; Calcium 57mg; Fibre 1.2g; Sodium 89mg.

Mini lamingtons

These are a traditional Australian treat. The sponge must be moist, but incredibly airy and fluffy. The chocolate glaze and crumbly coconut brings it all together to form a light, sweet delight.

MAKES 12–15

FOR THE CAKE
butter, for greasing
3 eggs
100g/3¹/₂oz/¹/₂ cup caster (superfine) sugar
100g/3¹/₂oz/³/₄ cup self-raising (self-rising) flour
35g/1¹/₂oz/¹/₃ cup cornflour (cornstarch)
15g/¹/₂oz/1 tbsp butter, melted
45ml/3 tbsp hot water
300g/11oz/2³/₄ cups desiccated (dry unsweetened shredded) coconut

FOR THE ICING
15g/¹/₂oz/1 tbsp butter
375g/13oz/3¹/₄ cups icing (confectioners') sugar, sifted
150g/5oz dark (bittersweet) chocolate (55% cocoa solids), chopped
90ml/6 tbsp full cream (whole) milk

1 Preheat the oven to 160°C/325°F/Gas 3. Butter a 20 x 30cm/8 x 12in cake tin (pan) and line with baking parchment. Beat the eggs until they begin to froth, then add the sugar. Beat until light and fluffy. Sift the flour and cornflour over the eggs and fold together with a rubber spatula or metal spoon.

2 Combine the butter and hot water in a measuring jug (cup) and fold into the mixture. Pour into the prepared tin (pan) and bake for 25–30 minutes, until just set. Leave to cool for 10 minutes before turning on to a rack. When cooled, cut the cake into 12–15 pieces. Put the coconut in a shallow dish.

3 To make the icing, put all the ingredients into a heatproof bowl over a pan of simmering water. Using a whisk, beat constantly to make an emulsified icing. Remove from the heat, but leave the bowl over the hot water.

4 With a dipping fork, dip each piece of cake into the icing. Wipe the bottom of the cake along the edge of the bowl to remove excess icing. Gently place the dipped cake into the coconut and turn to coat. Place the lamingtons on a clean wire rack and leave to set for about 15 minutes. Serve immediately, or store in an airtight container for up to 3 days.

Nutritional information per bar: Energy 365kcal/1530kJ; Protein 4.1g; Carbohydrate 48.7g, of which sugars 40.9g; Fat 18.4g, of which saturates 13.9g; Cholesterol 48mg; Calcium 53mg; Fibre 2.9g; Sodium 46mg.

Almond cream buns

These buns are meltingly delicious. The recipe can incorporate ready-made marzipan, but an even better idea is to make your own using the almond paste recipe shown below.

MAKES 12

275ml/16fl oz/2 cups double (heavy) cream
100g/4oz/¹/₂ cup unsalted butter
40g/1¹/₂oz fresh yeast
5ml/1 tsp ground cardamom
30ml/2 tbsp sugar
450g/1lb/4 cups plain (all-purpose) flour
a pinch of salt
1 egg, beaten
icing (confectioners') sugar, to decorate
warmed full cream (whole) milk , to serve

FOR THE FILLING

100g/4oz marzipan or almond paste (see below)
275ml/16fl oz/2 cups double (heavy) cream

FOR THE ALMOND PASTE (OPTIONAL)

100g/4oz/³/₄ cup blanched almonds
100g/4oz/¹/₂ cup icing (confectioners') sugar
¹/₂ egg white

1 If you want to make almond paste to replace the marzipan, put the almonds in a food processor or blender and, using a pulsating action, chop until finely ground. Add the sugar and egg white and mix to form a paste. The prepared almond paste can then be stored in a plastic bag in the refrigerator for up to 3 days until required.

2 Pour the cream into a pan and heat gently until warm to the touch. In a separate pan, gently melt the butter.

3 In a large bowl, blend the yeast with a little of the warmed cream and then add the melted butter, cardamom and sugar. Add the flour and salt and mix together to form a dough.

4 Turn the dough on to a lightly floured surface and knead for about 10 minutes until the dough feels firm and elastic. Shape into a ball, put in a clean bowl and cover with a clean dish towel. Leave to rise in a warm place for about 1¹/₂ hours until the dough has doubled in size.

5 Turn the dough on to a lightly floured surface and knead again for 2–3 minutes. Divide the dough into 12 equal pieces. Shape each piece into a round bun and place on a greased baking sheet. Cover with a clean dish towel and leave to rise in a warm place until doubled in size.

6 Preheat the oven to 180°C/350°F/Gas 4. Brush the tops of the buns with beaten egg to glaze then bake in the oven for about 10 minutes until golden brown. Transfer to a wire rack and leave to cool.

7 To serve, cut the tops off the buns and reserve. Remove about half of the dough from the buns and put in a bowl. Grate the marzipan or almond paste into the bowl and mix together. Replace the mixture in the buns.

8 Whisk the cream until stiff, top the buns with the whipped cream and then replace the tops. Sprinkle the icing sugar on top of each bun and serve.

Nutritional information per bun: Energy 465kcal/1938kJ; Protein 5.3g; Carbohydrate 38.2g, of which sugars 9.6g; Fat 33.4g, of which saturates 19.9g; Cholesterol 96mg; Calcium 85mg; Fibre 1.3g; Sodium 69mg.

Coconut cakes

These popular, moist coconut cakes are similar to coconut macaroons. They are best served straight from the oven, but also keep reasonably well in the freezer or in an airtight container.

MAKES 15–20

1 vanilla pod (bean)
120ml/4fl oz/½ cup double (heavy) cream
200g/7oz desiccated (dry unsweetened shredded) coconut
200g/4oz/1 cup caster (superfine) sugar
1 egg

1 Split open the vanilla pod and put in a pan with the cream. Heat gently until bubbles start to form round the edge of the pan then remove and leave to infuse for 20 minutes.

2 Preheat the oven to 200°C/400°F/Gas 6. Line a baking sheet with baking parchment. Remove the vanilla pod from the cream and pour the cream into a bowl.

3 Add the coconut, sugar and egg to the bowl and mix together.

4 Spoon the mixture in piles on to the prepared baking sheet. Bake in the oven for 12–15 minutes until the cakes are golden brown and a little crisp on top.

5 Leave the cakes to cool slightly before transferring to a cooling rack.

Nutritional information per cake: Energy 177kcal/740kJ; Protein 1.4g; Carbohydrate 14.9g, of which sugars 14.9g; Fat 13g, of which saturates 9.9g; Cholesterol 23.6mg; Calcium 16mg; Fibre 1.8g; Sodium 10.9mg.

Custard tarts

These tarts are delightful served with a small strong mid-morning coffee or with a refreshing cup of tea in the afternoon, and ensure a memorable in-between-meals snack.

MAKES 12

225g/8oz ready-made puff pastry, thawed if frozen
175ml/6fl oz/³/₄ cup fresh ready-made custard
30ml/2 tbsp icing (confectioners') sugar

1 Preheat the oven to 200°C/400°F/Gas 6. Roll out the pastry and cut out twelve 13cm/5in rounds. Line a 12-hole muffin tin (pan) with the pastry rounds. Line each round with a circle of baking parchment and some baking beans or uncooked rice.

2 Bake the tarts for 10–15 minutes, or until the pastry is cooked through and golden.

3 Remove the paper and baking beans or rice and set aside to cool.

4 Spoon the custard into the pastry cases and dust with the icing sugar.

5 Place the tarts under a preheated hot grill (broiler) and cook until the sugar caramelizes. Remove the tarts from the heat and leave to cool before serving.

Nutritional information per tart: Energy 94kcal/395kJ; Protein 1.5g; Carbohydrate 11.9g, of which sugars 4.7g; Fat 4.9g, of which saturates 0g; Cholesterol 0mg; Calcium 26mg; Fibre 0g; Sodium 64mg.

Chocolate éclairs

Many of the éclairs sold in French cake shops are filled with crème pâtissière. Here, the crisp choux pastry fingers are filled with fresh cream, slightly sweetened and flavoured with vanilla.

MAKES 12

300ml/½ pint/1¼ cups double (heavy) cream
10ml/2 tsp icing (confectioners') sugar, sifted
1.5ml/¼ tsp vanilla extract
115g/4oz plain (semisweet) chocolate
30ml/2 tbsp water
25g/1oz/2 tbsp butter

FOR THE PASTRY

65g/2½oz/9 tbsp plain (all-purpose) flour
a pinch of salt
50g/2oz/¼ cup butter, diced
150ml/¼ pint/⅔ cup water
2 eggs, lightly beaten

1 Preheat the oven to 200°C/400°F/Gas 6. Grease a baking sheet, line with baking parchment and dust with flour. Sift the flour and salt on to a sheet of parchment. Heat the butter and water until the butter melts. Increase the heat and bring to a rolling boil. Remove from the heat and beat in the flour.

2 Return the pan to low heat, then beat the mixture until it leaves the sides of the pan and forms a ball. Set the pan aside and cool for 2–3 minutes. Add the eggs, a little at a time until you have a smooth, shiny paste, thick enough to hold its shape.

3 Spoon the choux pastry into a piping (pastry) bag with a 2.5cm/1in plain nozzle. Pipe 10cm/4in lengths on to the prepared baking sheet. Use a wet knife to cut off the pastry at the nozzle.

4 Bake for 25–30 minutes, or until the pastries are well risen and golden brown. Remove from the oven and make a neat slit along the side of each to release the steam. Lower the oven temperature to 180°C/350°F/Gas 4 and bake for a further 5 minutes. Cool on a wire rack.

5 To make the filling, whip the cream with the icing sugar and vanilla extract until it just holds its shape. Spoon into a piping bag fitted with a 1cm/½in plain nozzle and use to fill the éclairs.

6 Place the chocolate and water in a small bowl over a pan of hot water. Melt, stirring, until smooth. Remove and stir in the butter. Dip the top of each éclair in the chocolate, then place on a wire rack. Leave the chocolate to set. The eclairs are best served within 2 hours of being made.

Nutritional information per éclair: Energy 253kcal/1050kJ; Protein 2.5g; Carbohydrate 11.6g, of which sugars 7.4g; Fat 22.2g, of which saturates 13.5g; Cholesterol 80mg; Calcium 29mg; Fibre 0.4g; Sodium 56mg.

Fruit loaf

An effective way for poor populations to create a sweet treat was to combine dried fruit with a bread recipe. Fruit loaf still remains a popular choice – serve the slices with butter and jam.

MAKES 1 LOAF

500g/1¼lb/generous 4 cups strong
   white bread flour, plus extra for dusting
2 sachets easy-blend (rapid-rise) dried
   yeast
250ml/8fl oz/1 cup lukewarm full cream
   (whole) milk
50g/2oz/¼ cup caster (superfine) sugar
a pinch of ground cinnamon
a pinch of freshly grated nutmeg
a pinch of powdered saffron
1 egg yolk, lightly beaten
50g/2oz/¼ cup butter, softened, plus
   extra for greasing
10ml/2 tsp salt
150g/5oz/⅔ cup currants
150g/5oz/1 cup raisins
50g/2oz/⅓ cup finely diced glacé
   (candied) citron peel
50g/2oz/⅓ cup glacé (candied) orange
   peel

1 Sift the flour into a bowl. Add the yeast and some of the milk and mix. Add 5ml/1 tsp of sugar, cover with a dish towel and leave for 10 minutes.

2 Add the cinnamon, nutmeg and saffron to the remaining milk, add to the bowl and mix. Add the egg yolk, the remaining sugar and the butter, knead briefly, and add the salt.

3 Knead the dough on a lightly floured surface for 15 minutes, until it is not sticky and is full of little bubbles. Add extra milk if necessary.

4 Shape the dough into a ball, return to a clean bowl and cover. Leave for 1 hour, until doubled.

5 Poach the currants and raisins in simmering water for 10 minutes. Drain well and pat dry in a cloth.

6 Knead the dried fruit and the peel into the dough. Roll into a rectangle 30cm/12in wide. Roll it up, starting wherever the filling is most sparse.

7 Grease a 30 x 10 x 10cm/12 x 10 x 10in loaf tin (pan). Put the dough roll in the tin, the fold underneath. Cover with a dampened dish towel and leave for 1 hour. Preheat the oven to 200°C/400°F/Gas 6.

8 Bake the loaf for 35 minutes, brush with cold water and return to the oven for 1 minute. Turn out on to a wire rack.

Nutritional information per loaf: Energy 3375kcal/14303kJ; Protein 57.3g; Carbohydrate 705.8g, of which sugars 324.8g; Fat 55.2g, of which saturates 28.6g; Cholesterol 308mg; Calcium 1098mg; Fibre 26.2g; Sodium 4651mg.

Coffee and walnut Swiss roll

Often used as a pair, coffee and walnuts have a natural affinity. Here they appear together in a light and fluffy sponge rolled around a smooth orange liqueur cream mixture.

SERVES 6

10ml/2 tsp ground coffee, e.g. mocha orange-flavoured

15ml/1 tbsp near-boiling water

3 eggs

75g/3oz/scant 1/2 cup caster (superfine) sugar, plus extra for dusting

75g/3oz/2/3 cup self-raising (self-rising) flour

50g/2oz/1/2 cup toasted walnuts, finely chopped

FOR THE COINTREAU CREAM

115g/4oz/generous 1/2 cup caster (superfine) sugar

50ml/2fl oz/1/4 cup cold water

2 egg yolks

115g/4oz/8 tbsp unsalted butter, softened

15ml/1 tbsp Cointreau

1 Preheat the oven to 200°C/400°F/ Gas 6. Grease and line a 33 x 23cm/ 13 x 9in Swiss roll tin (jelly roll pan) with non-stick baking parchment.

2 Put the coffee in a bowl and pour the hot water over. Infuse for about 4 minutes, then strain through a sieve.

3 Whisk the eggs and sugar in a bowl until pale and thick. Sift the flour over and fold in with the coffee and walnuts. Turn into the tin and bake for 10–12 minutes.

4 Put on baking parchment sprinkled with caster sugar, peel off the paper and cool for 2 minutes.

5 Trim the edges then roll up from one of the short ends, with the baking parchment where the filling will be. Leave to cool.

6 Heat the sugar in the water over a low heat until dissolved. Boil rapidly until the syrup reaches 105°C/220°F on a sugar thermometer. Pour the syrup over the egg yolks, whisking, until thick and mousse-like. Add the butter, then whisk in the orange liqueur. Leave to cool and thicken.

7 Unroll the sponge and spread with the Cointreau cream. Re-roll and place on a plate seam-side down. Dust with caster sugar and chill.

Nutritional information per portion: Energy 440kcal/1840kJ; Protein 7g; Carbohydrate 44g, of which sugars 35g; Fat 27g, of which saturates 12g; Cholesterol 224mg; Calcium 85mg; Fibre 1.0g; Sodium 210mg.

Walnut and date cake

This is a wonderfully rich and moist cake perfect for afternoon tea. The dates are first soaked before being added to the cake mixture. Their inclusion gives the cake a delightfully succulent texture.

MAKES 1 CAKE

225g/8oz/1⅓ cups chopped dates
250ml/8fl oz/1 cup boiling water
5ml/1 tsp bicarbonate of soda (baking soda)
225g/8oz/generous 1 cup caster (superfine)
  sugar
1 egg, beaten
275g/10oz/2¼ cups plain (all-purpose) flour
2.5ml/½ tsp salt

75g/3oz/6 tbsp butter, softened
5ml/1 tsp vanilla extract
5ml/1 tsp baking powder
50g/2oz/½ cup chopped walnuts

1 Put the chopped dates into a warm, dry bowl and pour the boiling water over the top; it should just cover the dates. Add the bicarbonate of soda and mix in thoroughly. Leave to stand for 5–10 minutes.

2 Preheat the oven to 180°C/350°F/Gas 4. Lightly grease a 23 x 30cm/9 x 12in cake tin (pan) and line with baking parchment.

3 In a separate mixing bowl, combine all the remaining ingredients for the cake. Then mix in the dates, along with the soaking water until you have created a thick batter. You may find it necessary to add a little more boiling water to help the consistency.

4 Pour or spoon the batter into the tin and bake in the oven for 45 minutes. Remove from the oven and cool. Cut into thick wedges and serve.

Nutritional information per portion: Energy 749kcal/3155kJ; Protein 10.5g; Carbohydrate 125.5g, of which sugars 77.8g; Fat 26.2g, of which saturates 11g; Cholesterol 88mg; Calcium 153mg; Fibre 3.4g; Sodium 141mg.

Black Forest gateau

Famous all over the world, this cake hails from Germany. It's extremely decadent, full of chocolate, cream and Kirsch, and is a real dinner-party classic.

SERVES 12

100g/3½oz plain (semisweet) chocolate
100g/3½oz/7 tbsp butter, softened
100g/3½oz/½ cup caster (superfine) sugar
10ml/2 tsp vanilla extract or 20g/¾oz vanilla sugar
6 eggs, separated
a pinch of salt
100g/3½oz/¾ cup plain (all-purpose) flour
50g/2oz/½ cup cornflour (cornstarch)
5ml/1 tsp baking powder

FOR THE FILLING

500g/1¼lb bottled cherries
5 gelatine leaves, soaked in cold water for 5 minutes
750ml/1¼ pints/3 cups double (heavy) cream
5ml/1 tsp vanilla extract or 5g/⅛oz vanilla sugar
100ml/3½ fl oz/scant ½ cup Kirsch

TO DECORATE

12 glacé (candied) cherries
75g/3oz flaked chocolate

1 Break up the chocolate and melt it in a bowl over a pan of simmering water. Preheat the oven to 160°C/325°F/Gas 3. Butter a 30cm/12in cake tin (pan).

2 Cream the butter with the sugar and vanilla extract or vanilla sugar. Gradually beat in the egg yolks, until light and foamy. Mix in the melted chocolate. Beat the egg whites with a pinch of salt until stiff and fold them into the mixture. Sift the flour and cornflour with the baking powder and fold in. Turn the mixture into the prepared tin and bake for 45–60 minutes, until a skewer pushed into the centre comes out clean. Leave to cool a little in the tin, then take out and leave on a rack to cool completely.

3 Strain the juice from the cherries into a pan. Bring to the boil, remove from the heat and add the gelatine. Stir until the gelatine has dissolved. Leave to cool. Whip the cream with the vanilla until stiff.

4 Slice the cake into three layers. Sprinkle the bottom layer with half the Kirsch, then spread half of the cherry jelly over it and put half the cherries on top. Top with some cream. Put the second layer of cake on top, and repeat the layers of Kirsch, jelly, cherries and cream. Top with the final cake.

5 Spread cream around the sides of the cake, and pipe 12 whirls on the top. Add a glacé cherry to each. Sprinkle flaked chocolate on top of the cake and press the rest into the sides. Chill for 5 hours. Serve.

Nutritional information per portion: Energy 551kcal/2293kJ; Protein 5.7g; Carbohydrate 36.8g, of which sugars 26.2g; Fat 45.7g, of which saturates 25.5g; Cholesterol 196mg; Calcium 73mg; Fibre 0.5g; Sodium 128mg.

Frosted carrot and parsnip cake

The carrots and parsnips in this deliciously light and crumbly cake help to keep it moist. The creamy sweetness of the cooked meringue topping contrasts with the cake's light crumb.

SERVES 8

grated rind of 1 lemon
grated rind and juice of 1 orange
15ml/1 tbsp caster (superfine) sugar
225g/8oz/1 cup butter
225g/8oz/1 cup soft light brown sugar
4 eggs
225g/8oz/1²⁄₃ cups mixed carrots
   and parsnips, grated
115g/4oz/1¼ cups sultanas
   (golden raisins)
225g/8oz/2 cups self-raising (self-rising)
   wholemeal (whole-wheat) flour, sifted
   with 5ml/1 tsp baking powder

FOR THE TOPPING
50g/2oz/¼ cup caster (superfine) sugar
1 egg white
a pinch of salt

1 Preheat the oven to 180°C/350°F/ Gas 4. Lightly grease a 20cm/8in loose-based cake tin (pan) and line the base with baking parchment.

2 Put half the lemon and orange rind in a bowl and mix with the caster sugar. Arrange the sugar-coated rind on baking parchment and leave to dry.

3 Cream the butter and sugar, then beat in the eggs. Stir in the unsugared rinds, grated carrots and parsnips, sultanas and 30ml/2 tbsp orange juice. Gradually fold in the flour and baking powder, and put into the tin.

4 Bake for 1¹⁄₂ hours until golden and just firm. Leave to cool slightly in the tin, then turn out on to a plate to cool.

5 For the topping, place the sugar in a bowl over boiling water with 30ml/ 2 tbsp of the orange juice. Stir over the heat until the sugar dissolves. Off the heat, add the egg white and salt, and whisk for 1 minute. Return to the heat and whisk for 6 minutes until stiff and glossy. Allow to cool slightly.

6 Swirl the topping over the cake and leave to firm up for 1 hour. Sprinkle with the sugared rind to decorate.

Nutritional information per portion: Energy 414kcal/1734kJ; Protein 6.2g; Carbohydrate 52.8g, of which sugars 38.9g; Fat 21.3g, of which saturates 12.4g; Cholesterol 124mg; Calcium 47mg; Fibre 2.3g; Sodium 175mg.

Gingerbread

Gingerbread is a winner at Christmas or for more everyday treats. It is flavoured with cloves, cinnamon, ginger, cardamom, allspice and nutmeg, here bought as Lebkuchen mix.

MAKES 30 SQUARES

300g/11oz/scant 3 cups hazelnuts
300g/11oz/1½ cups soft light brown sugar
5 eggs
150g/5oz/10 tbsp butter, melted
100g/3½oz/½ cup honey
500g/1¼lb/5 cups plain (all-purpose) flour
25ml/5 tsp baking powder
25g/1oz Lebkuchen spice mix

1 Preheat the oven to 160°C/325°F/Gas 3 and line a 40 x 30cm/16 x 12in baking tray with baking parchment.

2 Heat a frying pan over medium heat and toast the hazelnuts, moving them around constantly so that they brown evenly. Remove from the heat, cool, then chop finely.

3 Beat the sugar with the eggs until the mixture is light and thick. Stir in the butter, the honey and the chopped hazelnuts. Sift the flour with the baking powder and spice mix and fold into the mixture.

4 Pour the batter into the prepared tray. Bake in the preheated oven for about 45 minutes. Leave to cool before cutting into squares.

Nutritional information per square: Energy 741kcal/3106kJ; Protein 14.1g; Carbohydrate 89.1g, of which sugars 45.4g; Fat 38.9g, of which saturates 11.5g; Cholesterol 144mg; Calcium 166mg; Fibre 3.8g; Sodium 171mg

White chocolate mousse and strawberry layer cake

Make this spectacular cake in summer, when strawberries are at their most tasty. This would be an unforgettable choice for a special celebratory garden party.

SERVES 10

115g/4oz white chocolate, chopped into
    small pieces
120ml/4fl oz/^{1}/$_2$ cup double
    (heavy) cream
120ml/4fl oz/^{1}/$_2$ cup full cream (whole) milk
15ml/1 tbsp rum or vanilla extract
115g/4oz/^{1}/$_2$ cup unsalted butter, softened
175g/6oz/^{3}/$_4$ cup sugar
3 eggs
225g/8oz/2 cups plain (all-purpose) flour
10ml/2 tsp baking powder
a pinch of salt

675g/1^1/$_2$lb fresh strawberries, sliced, plus
    extra for decoration
750ml/1^1/$_4$ pints/3 cups whipping cream
30ml/2 tbsp rum or strawberry liqueur

**FOR THE WHITE CHOCOLATE
MOUSSE FILLING**

250g/9oz white chocolate, chopped into
    small pieces
350ml/12fl oz/1^1/$_2$ cups double
    (heavy) cream
30ml/2 tbsp rum or strawberry liqueur

1 Preheat the oven to 180°C/350°F/Gas 4. Grease and flour two 23cm/9in cake tins (pans). Line the bases with baking parchment. Melt the chocolate and cream in a double boiler over a low heat, stirring until smooth. Stir in the milk and rum or vanilla extract, and set aside to cool.

2 In a large mixing bowl, beat the butter and sugar with a hand-held electric mixer for 3–5 minutes, until light and creamy, scraping the sides of the bowl occasionally. Add the eggs one at a time, beating well after each addition. In a small bowl, stir together the flour, baking powder and salt. Alternately add flour and melted chocolate to the egg mixture in batches, until just blended. Pour the mixture into the tins and spread evenly.

3 Bake for 20–25 minutes, until a skewer inserted in the cakes comes out clean. Cool in the tins for 10 minutes, then turn the cakes out on to a wire rack, peel off the paper and cool completely.

4 Make the mousse filling. In a medium pan over a low heat, melt the chocolate and cream until smooth, stirring frequently. Stir in the rum or strawberry liqueur and pour into a bowl. Cool, then chill until just set. With a wire whisk, whip lightly.

5 With a serrated knife, slice both cake layers in half, making four layers. Place one layer on the plate and spread one-third of the mousse on top. Arrange one-third of the sliced strawberries over the mousse. Place the second layer on top and spread with another third of the mousse. Arrange another third of the strawberries over the mousse.

6 Place the third layer on top and spread with the remaining mousse. Cover with the remaining sliced strawberries. Top with the last cake layer. Whip the whipping cream with the rum or liqueur until firm peaks form. Spread the whipped cream over the top and sides of the cake. Halve the extra strawberries and use to decorate the cake.

Nutritional information per portion: Energy 1011kcal/4196kJ; Protein 10.3g; Carbohydrate 64.6g, of which sugars 47.4g; Fat 79g, of which saturates 48.3g; Cholesterol 227mg; Calcium 242mg; Fibre 1.4g; Sodium 171mg.

Baklava

This famous Middle Eastern dessert is traditionally made with eight layers of pastry dough and seven layers of chopped nuts. The classic baklava uses just walnuts, but fillings vary.

SERVES 12

175g/6oz/³/₄ cup clarified or plain butter, or
  sunflower oil
100ml/3¹/₂fl oz/scant ¹/₂ cup sunflower oil
450g/1lb filo sheets
450g/1lb walnuts, or a mixture of walnuts,
  pistachios and almonds, finely chopped
5ml/1 tsp ground cinnamon

FOR THE SYRUP

450g/1lb sugar
juice of 1 lemon, or 30ml/2 tbsp rose water

1 Preheat the oven to 160°C/325°F/Gas 3. Melt the butter and oil in a small pan, then brush a little over the bottom and sides of a 30cm/12in round or square cake tin (pan). Place a sheet of filo in the bottom and brush it with melted butter and oil. Continue until you have used half the filo sheets, brushing each one with butter and oil. Ease the sheets into the corners and trim the edges if they flop over the rim of the tin.

2 Spread the nuts over the last buttered sheet and sprinkle with the cinnamon, then continue as before with the remaining filo sheets. Brush the top one as well, then, using a sharp knife, cut diagonal parallel lines right through all the layers to the bottom to form small diamond shapes.

3 Bake in the oven for about 1 hour, until the top is golden – if it is still pale, increase the temperature for a few minutes at the end.

4 Meanwhile, make the syrup. Put the sugar into a heavy pan, pour in 250ml/8fl oz/1 cup water and bring to the boil, stirring all the time. When the sugar has dissolved, lower the heat and stir in the lemon juice or rose water, then simmer for about 15 minutes, until the syrup thickens. Leave to cool.

5 Remove the baklava from the oven and slowly pour the cooled syrup over the piping hot pastry. Return to the oven for 2–3 minutes to soak up the syrup, then take it out and leave to cool.

6 Once the baklava is cool, lift the pieces out of the tin and arrange them in a serving dish.

Nutritional information per portion: Energy 973kcal/4059kJ; Protein 12.2g; Carbohydrate 89.9g, of which sugars 60.9g; Fat 65.2g, of which saturates 15.6g; Cholesterol 47mg; Calcium 139mg; Fibre 3.1g; Sodium 141mg.

Satisfying Vegetarian Suppers

This collection of cheesy, creamy,

herb-infused sauces, simple pasta dishes and

richly spiced vegetable stews will ensure

that vegetarians suffer no hardships. Here

are recipes to convert the most hardened

meat-eaters, each one designed to create

meals to remember and make your mouth

water. The temptations include Creamy

Polenta with Dolcelatte, Mixed Bean and

Tomato Chilli, and Pumpkin, Rosemary

and Chilli Risotto.

Pasta with pesto

Bottled pesto is a useful stand-by, but it bears no resemblance to the heady aroma and flavour of the fresh paste. It is quick and easy to make in a food processor or blender.

SERVES 4

50g/2oz/1¹/₃ cups fresh basil leaves, plus extra, to garnish
2–4 garlic cloves
60ml/4 tbsp pine nuts
120ml/4fl oz/¹/₂ cup extra virgin olive oil
115g/4oz/1¹/₃ cups freshly grated Parmesan cheese, plus extra, shaved, to serve
25g/1oz/¹/₃ cup freshly grated Pecorino cheese
400g/14oz/3¹/₂ cups dried pasta
salt and ground black pepper

1 Put the basil leaves, garlic and pine nuts in a blender or food processor. Add 60ml/4 tbsp of the olive oil. Process until the ingredients are finely chopped, then stop the machine, remove the lid and scrape down the sides of the bowl.

2 Turn the machine on again and slowly pour the remaining oil in a steady stream through the feeder tube. You may need to stop the machine and scrape down the sides of the bowl once or twice to make sure everything is evenly mixed.

3 Scrape the mixture into a large bowl and beat in the Parmesan and Pecorino cheeses with a wooden spoon. Taste and add salt and pepper if necessary.

4 Cook the pasta according to the instructions on the packet.

5 Once cooked, drain the pasta, then add it to the bowl of pesto and toss well. Serve immediately, garnished with the fresh basil leaves. Hand a bowl of shaved Parmesan around separately.

Nutritional information per portion: Energy 713kcal/2969kJ; Protein 24.1g; Carbohydrate 43.2g, of which sugars 2.7g; Fat 50.5g, of which saturates 11.6g; Cholesterol 35mg; Calcium 468mg; Fibre 2.1g; Sodium 385mg.

Alfredo's fettuccine

This traditional, simple recipe was invented by a Roman restaurateur called Alfredo, who became famous for serving it with a gold fork and spoon. It is a supremely satisfying meal.

SERVES 4

50g/2oz/¼ cup butter
200ml/7fl oz/scant 1 cup panna da
   cucina or double (heavy) cream
50g/2oz/⅔ cup freshly grated Parmesan
   cheese, plus extra to serve
350g/12oz fresh fettuccine
salt and ground black pepper

1 Melt the butter in a large pan. Add the panna da cucina or double cream and bring to the boil.

2 Simmer for 5 minutes, stirring, add the Parmesan, salt and pepper to taste, and turn off the heat.

3 Bring a large pan of salted water to the boil. Drop in all the pasta and bring the pan back to the boil, stirring occasionally.

4 Cook the pasta until *al dente*: for approximately 2–3 minutes, or according to the instructions. Drain well.

5 Turn on the heat under the pan of cream to low, add all the cooked pasta and toss until it is well coated in the sauce. Taste for seasoning. Serve immediately, with extra grated Parmesan handed around separately.

Nutritional information per portion: Energy 697kcal/2912kJ; Protein 16.3g; Carbohydrate 65.8g, of which sugars 3.8g; Fat 42.8g, of which saturates 26g; Cholesterol 108mg; Calcium 199mg; Fibre 2.6g; Sodium 226mg.

Cheesy creamy leeks

Sometimes the easiest recipe is the most comforting, with a short, fuss-free preparation and maximum enjoyment. This makes a filling supper when accompanied by brown rice or couscous.

SERVES 4

**4 large leeks or 12 baby leeks, trimmed
and washed**
15ml/1 tbsp olive oil
**150ml/¼ pint/⅔ cup double (heavy)
cream**
**75g/3oz mature (sharp) Cheddar or
Monterey Jack cheese, grated**
salt and ground black pepper

1 Preheat the grill (broiler) to high. If using large leeks, slice them lengthways. Heat the oil in a large frying pan and add the leeks. Season with salt and pepper and cook for about 4 minutes, stirring occasionally, until starting to turn golden.

2 Pour the cream into the pan and stir until well combined. Allow to bubble gently for a few minutes.

3 Preheat the grill (broiler). Transfer the creamy leeks to a shallow ovenproof dish and sprinkle with the cheese. Grill (broil) for 4–5 minutes, or until the cheese is golden brown and bubbling, and serve immediately.

Nutritional information per portion: Energy 322kcal/1330kJ; Protein 7.8g; Carbohydrate 5g, of which sugars 4g; Fat 29.8g, of which saturates 17.1g; Cholesterol 70mg; Calcium 193mg; Fibre 3.3g; Sodium 147mg.

Creamy polenta with Dolcelatte

Here is another recipe with a minimum of ingredients that can be prepared in less than ten minutes. Soft-cooked polenta makes a delicious change from the usual potatoes or rice.

SERVES 4–6

900ml/1½ pints/3¾ cups full cream (whole) milk
115g/4oz/1 cup instant polenta
115g/4oz Dolcelatte cheese
60ml/4 tbsp extra virgin olive oil
salt and ground black pepper

1 Pour the milk into a large pan and bring to the boil, then add a good pinch of salt. Remove the pan from the heat and pour in the polenta in a slow, steady stream, stirring constantly to combine.

2 Return the pan to a low heat and simmer gently, stirring constantly, for 5 minutes. Remove the pan from the heat and stir in the olive oil.

3 Spoon the polenta into a serving dish and crumble the cheese over the top. Season with more ground black pepper and serve immediately.

Nutritional information per portion: Energy 271kcal/1131kJ; Protein 10.8g; Carbohydrate 21.1g, of which sugars 7.1g; Fat 16.1g, of which saturates 6.3g; Cholesterol 23mg; Calcium 274mg; Fibre 0.4g; Sodium 298mg.

Pasta with roast tomatoes and goat's cheese

The sweetness of roasted tomatoes contrasts perfectly with the sharp taste and creamy texture of goat's cheese, a delightful taste of the mediterranean. Serve with a crisp, green salad.

SERVES 4

8 large ripe tomatoes
60ml/4 tbsp garlic-infused olive oil
450g/1lb any dried pasta shapes
200g/7oz firm goat's cheese, crumbled
salt and ground black pepper

1 Preheat the oven to 190°C/375°F/Gas 5. Remove the tomato stalks and cut the tomatoes in half.

2 Place the tomatoes, cut side up, in a roasting pan and drizzle over 30ml/2 tbsp of the oil. Season well with salt and pepper and roast in the oven for 20–25 minutes, or until soft and slightly charred.

3 Meanwhile, cook the pasta in plenty of salted, boiling water, according to the instructions on the packet. Drain well and return to the pan.

4 Roughly mash the tomatoes in the roasting pan with a fork, and stir the contents of the roasting pan into the pasta. Gently stir in the goat's cheese along with the remaining oil and serve.

Nutritional information per portion: Energy 749kcal/3156kJ; Protein 28g; Carbohydrate 95g, of which sugars 12g; Fat 31g, of which saturates 13g; Cholesterol 49mg; Calcium 419mg; Fibre 6.5g; Sodium 500mg.

Macaroni cheese

Rich and creamy, this is a deluxe version of macaroni cheese, and is guaranteed to lift your spirits. It goes well with either a tomato and basil salad or a leafy green salad.

SERVES 4

250g/9oz/2¼ cups short-cut macaroni
50g/2oz/¼ cup butter
50g/2oz/½ cup plain (all-purpose) flour
600ml/1 pint/2½ cups full cream (whole) milk
100ml/3½ fl oz/scant ½ cup panna da cucina or double (heavy) cream
100ml/3½ fl oz/scant ½ cup dry white wine
50g/2oz/½ cup grated Gruyère or Emmenthal cheese
50g/2oz Fontina cheese, diced small
50g/2oz Gorgonzola cheese, crumbled
75g/3oz/1 cup freshly grated Parmesan cheese
salt and ground black pepper

1 Preheat the oven to 180°C/350°F/Gas 4. Cook the pasta according to the instructions on the packet.

2 Meanwhile, gently melt the butter in a pan, add the flour and cook, stirring, for 1–2 minutes until smooth. Add the milk a little at a time, whisking vigorously after each addition. Stir in the panna da cucina or cream, then the dry white wine. Bring to the boil. Cook, stirring constantly, until the sauce thickens. Remove from the heat.

3 Add the Gruyère or Emmenthal, Fontina, Gorgonzola and about a third of the grated Parmesan to the sauce. Mix well, then season to taste.

4 Drain the pasta well and put it into a baking dish. Pour the sauce over the pasta and mix well, then sprinkle the remaining Parmesan over the top. Bake for 25–30 minutes or until golden brown. Serve hot.

Nutritional information per portion: Energy 743kcal/3104kJ; Protein 30.3g; Carbohydrate 52.1g, of which sugars 8.9g; Fat 45.4g, of which saturates 27.8g; Cholesterol 123mg; Calcium 673mg; Fibre 0.4g; Sodium 593mg.

Smoked aubergines in cheese sauce

This recipe is from Turkey, where it was originally created for one of the Ottoman sultans. It is a warming and nourishing dish that is popular with children. Serve it as a main dish for supper with chunks of fresh, crusty bread and a refreshing green salad.

SERVES 4

2 large aubergines (eggplants)
50g/2oz/¼ cup butter
30ml/2 tbsp plain (all-purpose) flour
600ml/1 pint/2½ cups full cream (whole)
    milk, plus extra if needed

115g/4oz Cheddar cheese,
    grated
salt and ground black pepper
freshly grated Parmesan cheese,
    for the topping

1 Preheat the oven to 200°C/400°F/Gas 6. Put the aubergines directly on the gas flame on top of the stove, or under a conventional grill (broiler), and turn them until the skin is charred on all sides and the flesh feels soft. Place in a plastic bag and leave for a few minutes.

2 Hold each aubergine by the stalk under cold running water and gently peel off the charred skin.

3 Squeeze the flesh with your fingers to get rid of any excess water and place on a chopping board. Remove the stalks and chop the flesh to a pulp.

4 Make the sauce. Melt the butter in a heavy pan, remove from the heat and stir in the flour. Slowly beat in the milk, then return the pan to a medium heat and cook, stirring constantly, until the sauce is smooth and thick.

5 Beat in the grated Cheddar cheese a little at a time, then beat in the aubergine pulp and season with salt and pepper.

6 Transfer the mixture to a baking dish and sprinkle a generous layer of Parmesan over the top. Bake in the oven for about 25 minutes, until the top is nicely browned.

Nutritional information per portion: Energy 322kcal/1344kJ; Protein 14.1g; Carbohydrate 15.2g, of which sugars 9.3g; Fat 22.7g, of which saturates 14.5g; Cholesterol 63mg; Calcium 415mg; Fibre 2.2g; Sodium 350mg.

Mixed bean and tomato chilli

Here, mixed beans, fiery red chilli and fresh coriander are simmered in a tomato sauce to make a delicious vegetarian chilli. Serve with crusty bread or baked potatoes, and salad.

SERVES 4

400g/14oz jar tomato and herb sauce
2 x 400g/14oz cans mixed beans, drained and rinsed
1 fresh red chilli, seeded and sliced
a large handful of fresh coriander (cilantro), chopped
natural (plain) yogurt, to serve

1 Pour the tomato sauce and mixed beans into a pan. Reserve a little of the chilli and coriander, and add the remainder to the pan.

2 Bring the mixture to the boil, reduce the heat, cover and simmer gently for 10 minutes.

3 Stir the mixture occasionally and add a dash of water if the sauce starts to dry out.

4 Ladle the chilli into warmed individual serving bowls and top with a spoonful of yogurt and the reserved chilli and coriander.

Nutritional information per portion: Energy 309kcal/1302kj; Protein 16.7g; Carbohydrate 43.7g; of which sugars 14.1g; Fat 8.7g; of which saturates 4.2g; Cholesterol 18mg; Calcium 193g; Fibre 12.4g; Sodium 1202mg

Italian stuffed peppers

These flavourful peppers are easy to make for a light and healthy supper with friends, and are ideal served with a jacket potato, grated cheese and a mixed leaf green salad.

SERVES 4

10ml/2 tsp olive oil
1 red onion, sliced
1 courgette (zucchini), diced
115g/4oz/1½ cups mushrooms, sliced
1 garlic clove, crushed
400g/14oz can chopped tomatoes
15ml/1 tbsp tomato purée (paste)
30ml/2 tbsp torn fresh basil leaves
25g/1oz pine nuts (optional)
4 large (bell) peppers
25g/1oz/⅓ cup finely grated fresh
    Parmesan or Fontina cheese (optional)
salt and ground black pepper
fresh basil leaves and chopped fresh
    parsley, to garnish

1 Preheat the oven to 180°C/350°F/ Gas 4. Heat the oil in a non-stick pan, add the onion, courgette, mushrooms and garlic and cook gently for 3 minutes, stirring occasionally.

2 Stir in the tomatoes and tomato purée, then bring to the boil and simmer, uncovered, for 10–15 minutes until thickened slightly, stirring occasionally. Remove the pan from the heat and stir in the basil, seasoning and pine nuts, if using. Set aside.

3 Cut the peppers in half lengthways and deseed them. Blanch the pepper halves in boiling water for about 3 minutes. Drain. Place the peppers cut side up in a shallow ovenproof dish and fill with the vegetable mixture.

4 Cover the dish with foil and bake in the oven for 20 minutes. Uncover, sprinkle each pepper half with a little grated cheese, if using, and bake, uncovered, for a further 5–10 minutes. Garnish with parsley and basil leaves and serve immediately.

Nutritional information per portion of peppers: Energy 108kcal/450kJ; Protein 4.2g; Carbohydrate 17g, of which sugars 16.1g; Fat 2.9g, of which saturates 0.6g; Cholesterol 0mg; Calcium 40mg; Fibre 4.9g; Sodium 28mg.

Potato curry with yogurt

This simple Indian curry is traditionally served with a meat curry and rice, but it is also delicious on its own, served with bread and a spicy pickle or chutney. A dry version, without yogurt, can be used as a filling for flatbreads and pastries. For those who like a little heat, this will hit the spot.

SERVES 4

6 garlic cloves, chopped

25g/1oz root ginger, peeled and chopped

30ml/2 tbsp ghee

6 shallots, halved lengthways and sliced

2 green chillies, seeded and finely sliced

10ml/2 tsp sugar

a handful of fresh or dried curry leaves

2 cinnamon sticks

5–10ml/1–2 tsp ground turmeric

15ml/1 tbsp garam masala

500g/1¼lb waxy potatoes, diced

2 tomatoes, peeled, seeded and quartered

250ml/8fl oz/1 cup Greek (US strained plain) yogurt

salt and ground black pepper

5ml/1 tsp red chilli powder, and fresh coriander (cilantro) and mint leaves, finely chopped, to garnish

1 lemon, quartered, and flatbread, to serve

1 Using a mortar and pestle or a food processor, grind the garlic and ginger to a coarse paste.

2 Heat the ghee in a pan and stir in the shallots and chillies, until fragrant. Add the garlic and ginger paste with the sugar, and stir until the mixture begins to colour.

3 Stir in the curry leaves, cinnamon sticks, turmeric and garam masala, and toss in the potatoes, making sure they are well coated in the spice mixture.

4 Pour in enough cold water to cover the potatoes. Bring to the boil, then reduce to a simmer until the potatoes are just cooked – they should still have a bite to them.

5 Season with salt and pepper to taste. Gently toss in the tomatoes to heat them through. Fold in the yogurt so that it is streaky rather than completely mixed in. Sprinkle with the chilli powder, coriander and mint. Serve immediately from the pan, with lemon to squeeze over it and flatbread for scooping it up.

Nutritional information per portion: Energy 231kcal/967kJ; Protein 6.7g; Carbohydrate 26.2g, of which sugars 7.4g; Fat 12.4g, of which saturates 4.1g; Cholesterol 0mg; Calcium 110mg; Fibre 2g; Sodium 63mg.

Tagine of butter beans, tomatoes and olives

Serve this delightful tagine for maximum pleasure with a leafy salad and fresh, crusty bread.
For non-vegetarians you can include a spicy sausage like chorizo at the same stage as the onion.

SERVES 4

115g/4oz/²/₃ cup butter (lima) beans,
  soaked overnight
30–45ml/2–3 tbsp olive oil
1 onion, chopped
2–3 garlic cloves, crushed
25g/1oz fresh root ginger, peeled
  and chopped
a pinch of saffron threads
16 cherry tomatoes
a large pinch of sugar
a handful of fleshy black
  olives, pitted
5ml/1 tsp ground cinnamon
5ml/1 tsp paprika
a small bunch of flat leaf parsley,
  chopped
salt and ground black pepper

1 Rinse the beans and place them in a large pan with plenty of water. Bring to the boil and boil for about 10 minutes, then reduce the heat and simmer gently for 1–1½ hours until tender. Drain the beans and refresh under cold water.

2 Heat the olive oil in a heavy pan. Add the onion, garlic and ginger, and cook for about 10 minutes, or until softened but not browned. Stir in the saffron threads, followed by the cherry tomatoes and a sprinkling of sugar.

3 As the tomatoes begin to soften, stir in the butter beans. When the tomatoes have heated through, stir in the olives, ground cinnamon and paprika. Season to taste and sprinkle over the parsley. Serve immediately.

COOK'S TIP

If you are in a hurry, you could use two 400g/14oz cans of butter beans for this tagine. Make sure you rinse the beans well before adding as canned beans tend to be salty.

Nutritional information per portion: Energy 138kcal/578kJ; Protein 5.5g; Carbohydrate 12.8g, of which sugars 3.5g; Fat 7.6g, of which saturates 1.1g; Cholesterol 0mg; Calcium 51mg; Fibre 5.2g; Sodium 605mg.

Red lentil fritters

These spicy fritters come from the Indian subcontinent and can be used in a similar way to falafel. Serve with a crisp green salad, a wedge of lemon and a spoonful of fragrant mint chutney.

SERVES 4–6

250g/9oz/generous 1 cup red lentils, soaked overnight

3–5 garlic cloves, chopped

30ml/2 tbsp roughly chopped fresh root ginger

120ml/4fl oz/$\frac{1}{2}$ cup chopped fresh coriander (cilantro) leaves

2.5–5ml/$\frac{1}{2}$–1 tsp ground cumin

1.5–2.5ml/$\frac{1}{4}$–$\frac{1}{2}$ tsp ground turmeric

$\frac{1}{2}$–1 fresh red chilli, chopped

50g/2oz/$\frac{1}{2}$ cup gram flour

5ml/1 tsp baking powder

30ml/2 tbsp couscous

2 large or 3 small onions, chopped

vegetable oil, for deep-frying

salt and ground black pepper

green salad, lemon wedges and chutney, to serve

1 Drain the lentils. Put the garlic and ginger in a processor or blender and process until finely minced (ground). Add the lentils, 15–30ml/1–2 tbsp of water and the coriander, and process to a purée.

2 Add the cumin, turmeric, chilli, gram flour, baking powder and couscous to the mixture. Mix in the onions. Stir in the garlic purée and coriander and season.

3 Heat the oil in a large frying pan, to a depth of about 5cm/2in, until it is hot enough to brown a cube of bread in 30 seconds. Using two spoons, form the mixture into bitesize balls and slip each one into the hot oil. Cook in batches, on both sides, until golden brown.

4 Remove the fritters from the oil with a slotted spoon and drain on kitchen paper. Transfer the fritters to a baking sheet and keep warm in the oven until all the mixture is cooked. Serve hot.

Nutritional information per portion: Energy 291kcal/1226kJ; Protein 16.5g; Carbohydrate 38.8g, of which sugars 4.6g; Fat 8.6g, of which saturates 1g; Cholesterol 0mg; Calcium 115mg; Fibre 4g; Sodium 33mg.

Pumpkin, rosemary and chilli risotto

A dangerously rich and creamy risotto. The pumpkin gradually disintegrates to speckle the rice with orange. The rosemary gives it a sweet pungency, while garlic and chilli add bite.

SERVES 4

115g/4oz/¹/₂ cup butter
1 small onion, finely chopped
2 large garlic cloves, crushed
1 fresh red chilli, seeded and
    finely chopped
250g/9oz fresh pumpkin or butternut
    squash, peeled and roughly chopped
30ml/2 tbsp chopped fresh rosemary

250g/9oz/1¹/₂ cups risotto rice, preferably
    Arborio or Vialone Nano
about 750ml/1¹/₄ pints/3 cups hot vegetable
    stock, preferably fresh
50g/2oz/²/₃ cup freshly grated Parmesan
    cheese, plus extra to serve
salt and ground black pepper

1 Melt half the butter in a pan, add the onion and garlic, and cook for 10 minutes until soft. Add the chilli and cook for 1 minute. Add the pumpkin or squash and cook for 5 minutes. Stir in the rosemary.

2 Add the rice, and stir with a wooden spoon to coat with the oil and vegetables. Cook for 2–3 minutes to toast the rice grains.

3 Begin to add the stock, stirring in a ladleful at a time until it has been absorbed into the rice. The rice should always be bubbling slowly.

4 Continue adding the stock like this, stirring constantly, until the rice is tender and creamy, but the grains remain firm, and the pumpkin is beginning to disintegrate. (This should take about 20 minutes, depending on the type of rice used.) Taste and season well with salt and pepper.

5 Stir the remaining butter and the Parmesan cheese into the rice. Cover and let the risotto rest for 2–3 minutes. Serve the risotto with extra Parmesan cheese.

Nutritional information per portion: Energy 585kcal/2441kJ; Protein 14.4g; Carbohydrate 87.3g, of which sugars 5.7g; Fat 15.9g, of which saturates 3.5g; Cholesterol 8mg; Calcium 196mg; Fibre 3.2g; Sodium 151mg.

Comforting Fish and Meat Dishes

Here is a tempting range of heart-warming meals for fish and meat lovers. Fishy meals include Salt Cod Fritters with Aioli and Classic Fish and Chips, and sustaining meat options feature Corned Beef and Egg Hash, Roast Chicken with Baked Potatoes and Roasted Garlic and Lamb Stew in a Creamy Dill Sauce. If you have grey clouds shadowing you, then why not choose one of these dishes to bring some sunshine to your day?

Aromatic prawn laksa

This hearty dish is a marvellous pick-you-up. Combining tiger prawns, vegetables and noodles in a savoury coconut broth, the flavours and textures will soothe you and stimulate the appetite.

SERVES 4

6 dried red chillies
1 onion, chopped
1 small piece fresh root ginger, peeled
　　and grated
5ml/1 tsp ground turmeric
45ml/3 tbsp Thai fish sauce
finely grated rind of 1 lime
8 macadamia nuts
5ml/1 tsp ground coriander (cilantro)
60ml/4 tbsp vegetable oil
475ml/16fl oz/2 cups fish stock
750ml/1¼ pints/3 cups coconut milk
　　from a can or carton
225g/8oz dried flat rice noodles
120ml/4fl oz/½ cup coconut cream
400g/14oz raw headless tiger prawns
　　(jumbo shrimp), shelled and deveined
　　but with tails left intact
225g/8oz/4 cups fresh beansprouts
coriander (cilantro) sprigs, to serve

1 Soak the chillies in warm water for 30 minutes. Drain them, cut them in half and remove the seeds. Put the chillies, onion, ginger, turmeric, fish sauce, lime rind, macadamia nuts, ground coriander and half of the vegetable oil into a food processor or blender and process to form a smooth paste.

2 Heat the remaining oil in a pan, add the paste and fry for 5 minutes, stirring all the time to prevent sticking. Add the fish stock and simmer for a further 5 minutes.

3 Stir in the canned coconut milk. Bring to the boil and simmer, uncovered, for about 5 minutes, stirring constantly. Meanwhile, cook the noodles in a separate pan of boiling water according to the packet instructions, drain and toss in a little oil. Set aside.

4 Stir the coconut cream and prawns into the soup. Simmer for a further 2–3 minutes. To serve, put a pile of noodles into four deep serving bowls. Add the beansprouts and prawns, and pour over the hot soup. Top with the coriander and serve immediately.

Nutritional information per portion: Energy 324kcal/1354kJ; Protein 22g; Carbohydrate 18g, of which sugars 13g; Fat 19g, of which saturates 3g; Cholesterol 195mg; Calcium 166mg; Fibre 3.7g; Sodium 1173mg.

Niçoise noodle salad with seared tuna

Seared fresh tuna, egg noodles and crisp, colourful Mediterranean vegetables tossed with a herby garlic dressing creates an appealing combination of textures and a meal full of goodness.

SERVES 4

2 fresh tuna steaks, each weighing about 225g/8oz
175g/6oz fine green beans, trimmed
3 eggs
350g/12oz Chinese dried egg noodles
225g/8oz baby plum tomatoes, quartered
50g/2oz/½ cup small black olives
a handful of fresh basil leaves, torn
salt and ground black pepper

FOR THE MARINADE
30ml/2 tbsp lemon juice
75ml/5 tbsp olive oil
2 garlic cloves, crushed

FOR THE WARM DRESSING
90ml/6 tbsp extra virgin olive oil
30ml/2 tbsp wine vinegar or lemon juice
2 garlic cloves, crushed
2.5ml/½ tsp Dijon mustard
30ml/2 tbsp capers
45ml/3 tbsp chopped mixed herbs

1 To make the marinade, combine the lemon juice, olive oil and garlic in a dish. Add salt and pepper and mix well. Add the tuna and turn to coat in the marinade. Cover and leave to marinate in a cool place for 1 hour. Whisk all the ingredients for the dressing together in a small pan and leave to infuse.

2 Blanch the green beans in boiling salted water for 4 minutes. Drain and refresh in cold water. In a separate pan, cover the eggs with cold water. Bring to the boil, then boil for 10 minutes. Immediately drain and cover with cold water to stop the cooking. When cool, shell and quarter the eggs.

3 Put the noodles and blanched beans into a bowl and pour boiling water over to cover. Leave for 5 minutes, then fork up the noodles. Heat the dressing and keep warm. Drain the noodles and beans, and toss with the dressing.

4 Heat a ridged griddle pan or heavy skillet until smoking. Drain the tuna steaks, pat dry and sear for 1–2 minutes on each side. Remove and slice thinly. Add the tuna with the quartered tomatoes and olives to the noodles and beans, and toss well. Pile the salad into warmed bowls and sprinkle with the quartered eggs and basil. Season with salt and pepper and serve while warm.

Nutritional information per portion: Energy 578kcal/2408kJ; Protein 46.4g; Carbohydrate 15g, of which sugars 10.6g; Fat 37.5g, of which saturates 7.1g; Cholesterol 235mg; Calcium 127mg; Fibre 4.7g; Sodium 585mg.

Salt cod fritters with aioli

Bacalao – salt cod – is one of the great Spanish delights, adding flavour to bland ingredients such as potatoes. If you are unfamiliar with it, then this is a delightful way to try it out. Bitesize fish cakes, dipped into rich, creamy, garlicky aioli, are irresistible as a tapas dish or appetizer.

SERVES 6

450g/1lb salt cod
500g/1¼lb floury potatoes
300ml/½ pint/1¼ cups full cream
   (whole) milk
6 spring onions (scallions),
   finely chopped
30ml/2 tbsp extra virgin olive oil
30ml/2 tbsp chopped fresh parsley
juice of ½ lemon
2 eggs, beaten
plain (all-purpose) flour, for dusting
90g/3½oz/1¼ cups dried white
   breadcrumbs

olive oil, for shallow frying
salt and ground black pepper
lemon wedges and salad leaves, to serve

FOR THE AIOLI
2 large garlic cloves, finely chopped
2 egg yolks
300ml/½ pint/1¼ cups olive oil
juice of ½ lemon, to taste

1 Soak the salt cod in cold water for at least 24 hours, changing the water two or three times. The cod should swell as it rehydrates. Sample a tiny piece. It should not taste unpleasantly salty when fully rehydrated. Drain well and pat dry with kitchen paper.

2 Cook the potatoes, unpeeled, in a pan of lightly salted boiling water for about 20 minutes, until tender. Drain. As soon as they are cool enough to handle, peel the potatoes, then mash with a fork or potato masher.

3 Pour the milk into a pan, add half the spring onions and simmer. Add the soaked cod and poach gently for 10–15 minutes, until it flakes easily. Remove the cod and flake it with a fork into a bowl, discarding bones and skin.

4 Add 60ml/4 tbsp mashed potato to the cod and beat them together with a wooden spoon. Work in the olive oil, then gradually add the remaining mashed potato. Beat in the remaining spring onions and the parsley.

5 Season with lemon juice and pepper to taste – the mixture may also need a little salt but taste it before adding any. Add one beaten egg to the mixture and beat in until thoroughly combined, then chill until firm.

6 Shape the chilled fish mixture into 12–18 balls, then gently flatten into small round cakes. Coat each one in flour, then dip in the remaining beaten egg and coat with dried breadcrumbs. Chill until ready to fry.

7 Meanwhile, make the aioli. Place the garlic and a good pinch of salt in a mortar and pound to a paste with a pestle. Transfer to a bowl and gradually beat in the egg yolks with a whisk or wooden spoon.

8 Beat in about half the olive oil, a drop at a time. When the sauce is as thick as soft butter, beat in 5–10ml/1–2 tsp lemon juice. Continue adding oil until the aioli is very thick. Season to taste, adding more lemon juice if you wish.

9 Heat about 2cm/³⁄₄in oil in a large frying pan. Add the fritters and cook over a medium-high heat for about 4 minutes. Turn them over and cook for a further 4 minutes on the other side, until crisp and golden. Drain on kitchen paper, then serve with the aioli, lemon wedges and salad leaves.

Nutritional information per portion: Energy 653kcal/2721kJ; Protein 32.7g; Carbohydrate 28.1g, of which sugars 4.2g; Fat 46.4g, of which saturates 7.6g; Cholesterol 178mg; Calcium 123mg; Fibre 1.4g; Sodium 472mg.

Cod and bean stew

This stew is cooked in one pot – the chunks of fresh, flaky cod, made yellow with saffron, are added at the last minute, and their flavour is offset by the smoked paprika-spiced beans.

SERVES 6–8

1 large red (bell) pepper
45ml/3 tbsp olive oil
4 rashers (strips) streaky (fatty) bacon,
    roughly chopped
4 garlic cloves, finely chopped
1 onion, sliced
10ml/2 tsp paprika
5ml/1 tsp smoked Spanish paprika
a large pinch of saffron threads or 1
    sachet powdered saffron, soaked in
    45ml/3 tbsp hot water
400g/14oz jar Spanish butter (lima)
    beans or canned haricot (navy) beans
600ml/1 pint/2½ cups fish stock, or
    water and 60ml/4 tbsp Thai fish sauce
6 plum tomatoes, quartered
350g/12oz fresh skinned cod fillet, cubed
45ml/3 tbsp chopped fresh coriander
    (cilantro), plus a few sprigs to garnish
salt and ground black pepper
crusty bread, to serve

1 Preheat the grill (broiler) and line the pan with foil. Halve the red pepper and scoop out the seeds. Place, cut-side down, in the grill pan and grill (broil) under a high heat for about 10–15 minutes, until the skin is charred.

2 Put the pepper into a plastic bag, seal and leave for 10 minutes to steam. Remove, peel off the skin and discard. Chop the pepper into large pieces.

3 Heat the olive oil in a pan, then add the bacon and garlic. Fry for 2 minutes, then add the sliced onion. Cover the pan and cook for about 5 minutes until the onion is soft. Stir in the paprika and smoked Spanish paprika, the saffron and its soaking water, and salt and pepper.

4 Stir the beans into the pan and add enough stock to cover. Bring to the boil and simmer, uncovered, for about 15 minutes, stirring occasionally to prevent sticking. Stir in the chopped pepper, tomato quarters and cubes of cod. Cover and simmer for 5 minutes, until the fish flakes easily. Stir in the chopped coriander. Serve the stew in warmed soup plates or bowls, garnished with the coriander sprigs. Eat with crusty bread.

Nutritional information per portion: Energy 449kcal/1883kJ; Protein 44.5g; Carbohydrate 25.3g, of which sugars 3.9g; Fat 19.5g, of which saturates 3g; Cholesterol 84mg; Calcium 85mg; Fibre 9.8g; Sodium 403mg.

Classic fish and chips

This traditional British dish is delicious and wholesome when well cooked, and a marvellous way of burying the day's frustrations. The fish should be thick and succulent in fine crisp batter.

SERVES 4

450g/1lb potatoes
groundnut (peanut) oil, for deep-frying
4 x 175g/6oz cod fillets, skinned and any
   tiny bones removed
lemon halves, to serve

FOR THE BATTER
75g/3oz/²⁄₃ cup plain (all-purpose) flour
1 egg yolk
10ml/2 tsp vegetable oil
175ml/6fl oz/³⁄₄ cup water
salt

1 Cut the potatoes into 5mm/¼in thick slices. Cut the slices into 5mm/¼in chips. Rinse the chips in cold water, drain and then dry in a clean dishtowel. Heat the oil in a deep-fryer to 180°C/350°F. Add the chips and cook for 3 minutes, then remove from the pan and shake off all fat. Set to one side.

2 Sift the flour into a bowl. Add a pinch of salt. Make a well in the flour and place the egg yolk in this. Add the oil and some water. Mix and gradually add the remaining water, mixing in the flour. When combined, beat well until the batter is completely smooth. Cover and set aside until ready to use.

3 Cook the chips again in the fat for a further 5 minutes, until golden and crisp. Drain on kitchen paper and add salt. Keep hot while you cook the fish.

4 Dip the fish fillets into the batter and turn to ensure they are evenly coated. Allow excess batter to drip off before lowering the fish into the oil.

5 Cook the fish for 5 minutes, turning once, so that the batter browns evenly. Drain on kitchen paper. Serve at once, with lemon halves and the chips.

Nutritional information per portion: Energy 645kcal/2700kJ; Protein 32.6g; Carbohydrate 54.3g, of which sugars 0.7g; Fat 34.5g, of which saturates 3.5g; Cholesterol 38mg; Calcium 130mg; Fibre 3.4g; Sodium 294mg.

Fish pie with saffron and dill mash

This is the ultimate fish pie. Breaking through the golden potato crust reveals perfectly cooked plump prawns and hearty chunks of cod swathed in an irresistible creamy parsley sauce. Cook in a big dish and then bring it triumphantly to the table.

SERVES 6

750ml/1¼ pints/3 cups full cream (whole) milk
1 onion, chopped
1 bay leaf
2–3 peppercorns
450g/1lb each of fresh cod fillet and smoked haddock fillet, skin on
350g/12oz cooked tiger prawns (jumbo shrimp), shelled, with tails left on
75g/3oz/6 tbsp butter
75g/3oz/¾ cup plain (all-purpose) flour

60ml/4 tbsp chopped fresh parsley
salt and ground black pepper

FOR THE SAFFRON AND DILL MASH

1.3kg/3lb floury potatoes, peeled
a large pinch of saffron threads, soaked in 45ml/3 tbsp hot water
75g/3oz/6 tbsp butter
250ml/8fl oz/1 cup full cream (whole) milk
45ml/3 tbsp chopped fresh dill

1 Put the milk, onion, bay leaf and peppercorns into a large pan. Bring to the boil, then simmer for about 10 minutes. Set aside.

2 Lay the cod and haddock fillets, skin-side up, in a roasting pan. Strain over the milk and simmer for 5–7 minutes on the stovetop until just opaque. Lift the fish out of the milk and transfer to a plate. Reserve the milk.

3 When the fish is cool enough to handle, pull off the skin and flake the flesh into large pieces, removing any bones as you go. Transfer to a large bowl and add the shelled prawns.

4 Melt the butter in a small pan. Stir in the flour and cook for a minute or so, then gradually stir in the flavoured milk from the roasting pan until you achieve a smooth consistency. Whisk well and simmer gently for 15 minutes until thick and a little reduced, then taste and season with salt and pepper. Stir in the parsley.

5 Pour the sauce over the fish. Carefully mix them both together, transfer the mixture to a pie dish and leave it to cool.

6 Preheat the oven to 180°C/350°F/Gas 4. To make the saffron and dill mash, boil the potatoes in salted water until tender, drain well and mash, then press them through a sieve (strainer) to make sure they're really smooth.

7 Using an electric whisk, beat in the saffron and its soaking water, then the butter, milk and dill to make mashed potato that is light and fluffy. When the fish mixture has set, spoon over the golden mash, piling it on top. Bake for 30–40 minutes, or until the potato is golden brown and crisp. Serve hot.

Nutritional information per portion: Energy 458kcal/1921kJ; Protein 29.4g; Carbohydrate 32.8g, of which sugars 5.8g; Fat 25g, of which saturates 3.7g; Cholesterol 74mg; Calcium 216mg; Fibre 1g; Sodium 388mg.

Corned beef and egg hash

This American-style hash turns corned beef into a supper that is nursery food at its best! Make the mixture the day before and keep in the refrigerator so you can rustle it up quickly on the day.

SERVES 4

30ml/2 tbsp vegetable oil
25g/1oz/2 tbsp butter
1 onion, finely chopped
1 green (bell) pepper, seeded and diced
2 large firm boiled potatoes, diced
350g/12oz can corned beef, cubed
1.5ml/¼ tsp freshly grated nutmeg
1.5ml/¼ tsp paprika
4 eggs
salt and ground black pepper
deep-fried parsley, to garnish
sweet chilli sauce or tomato sauce, to
    serve

1 Heat the oil and butter together in a large frying pan. Add the onion and fry for 5–6 minutes until softened.

2 In a bowl, mix together the green pepper, potatoes, corned beef, nutmeg and paprika and season well. Add to the pan and toss gently to distribute the cooked onion. Press down lightly and fry without stirring on a medium heat for about 3–4 minutes until a golden brown crust has formed on the underside.

3 Stir the mixture through to distribute the crust, then repeat the frying twice, until the mixture is well browned.

4 Make four wells in the hash and carefully crack an egg into each. Cover and cook gently for about 4–5 minutes until the egg whites are set.

5 Sprinkle with deep-fried parsley and cut into quarters. Serve hot with sweet chilli sauce or tomato sauce.

Nutritional information per portion: Energy 419kcal/1748kJ; Protein 32g; Carbohydrate 13.6g, of which sugars 4.4g; Fat 27g, of which saturates 10.7g; Cholesterol 321mg; Calcium 74mg; Fibre 1.9g; Sodium 881mg.

Southern fried chicken

Fried chicken is now an international fast-food favourite that originated in America. This home-made version is substantial and tasty. Serve it with potato wedges to complete the meal.

SERVES 4

15ml/1 tbsp paprika
30ml/2 tbsp plain (all-purpose) flour
4 skinless, boneless chicken breast
    portions, each weighing 175g/6oz
30ml/2 tbsp sunflower oil
150ml/¹/₄ pint/²/₃ cup sour cream
15ml/1 tbsp chopped chives
salt and ground black pepper

FOR THE CORN CAKES
200g/7oz corn kernels
350g/12oz mashed potato, cooled
25g/1oz/2 tbsp butter

1 Mix the paprika and flour together. Coat each chicken breast in the flour.

2 Heat the oil in a large frying pan and add the chicken. Cook over a high heat until a golden brown colour. Reduce the heat and cook for 20 minutes more, turning once or twice, or until the chicken is cooked right through.

3 Stir the corn kernels into the cooled mashed potato and season with salt and pepper. Shape into 12 even-size round cakes, 5cm/2in in diameter.

4 When the chicken portions are cooked, use a slotted spoon to remove them from the pan and keep hot. Melt the butter in the pan and cook the corn cakes for 3 minutes on each side, or until golden and heated through.

5 Meanwhile, mix together the sour cream with the chives in a bowl to make a dip. Transfer the corn cakes from the frying pan to serving plates and top with the chicken breast portions. Serve at once, offering the sour cream with chives on the side.

Nutritional information per portion: Energy 505kcal/2119kJ; Protein 47.8g; Carbohydrate 32.2g, of which sugars 3.3g; Fat 21.5g, of which saturates 9.3g; Cholesterol 158mg; Calcium 61mg; Fibre 2.5g; Sodium 172mg.

Chicken and mushroom pie

This is a classic pie to bring a smile to the faces of diners of all ages. Porcini mushrooms intensify the flavour of the chicken and vegetables under the melt-in-the-mouth crust.

SERVES 6

15g/½oz/¼ cup dried porcini mushrooms
50g/2oz/¼ cup butter
30ml/2 tbsp plain (all-purpose) flour
250ml/8fl oz/1 cup hot chicken stock
60ml/4 tbsp single (light) cream
1 onion, coarsely chopped
2 carrots, sliced
2 celery sticks, coarsely chopped
50g/2oz/¾ cup fresh mushrooms, quartered
450g/1lb cooked chicken meat, cubed
50g/2oz/½ cup fresh or frozen peas

salt and ground black pepper
beaten egg, to glaze

FOR THE PASTRY
225g/8oz/2 cups plain (all-purpose) flour
1.5ml/¼ tsp salt
115g/4oz/½ cup cold butter, diced
65g/2½oz/⅓ cup white vegetable fat, diced
60–120ml/4–8 tbsp chilled water

1 To make the pastry, sift the flour and salt into a bowl. Cut or rub in the butter and white vegetable fat until the mixture resembles breadcrumbs. Sprinkle with 90ml/6 tbsp chilled water and mix until the dough holds together. If the dough is too crumbly, add a little more water, 15ml/1 tbsp at a time.

2 Gather the dough into a ball and flatten it into a round. Wrap and chill for at least 30 minutes.

3 Put the dried mushrooms in a bowl. Cover with hot water and soak for 30 minutes. Drain in a muslin- (cheesecloth-) lined sieve (strainer), then dry on kitchen paper. Preheat the oven to 190°C/375°F/Gas 5.

4 Melt half of the butter in a heavy pan. Whisk in the flour and cook until bubbling, whisking constantly. Add the hot stock and whisk over a medium heat until the mixture boils. Cook for 2–3 minutes, until it thickens, then whisk in the cream. Season to taste, and set aside.

5 Heat the remaining butter in a large, non-stick frying pan and cook the onion and carrots over a low heat for about 5 minutes. Add the celery and fresh mushrooms and cook for 5 minutes more. Stir in the cooked chicken, peas and drained porcini mushrooms.

6 Add the chicken mixture to the hot cream sauce and stir to mix. Adjust the seasoning if necessary. Spoon the mixture into a 2.5 litre/4 pint/2½ quart oval baking dish.

7 Roll out the pastry to a thickness of about 3mm/⅛in. Cut out an oval 2.5cm/1in larger all around than the dish. Lay the pastry over the filling. Gently press around the edge of the dish to seal, then trim off the excess pastry. Crimp the edge of the pastry by pushing the forefinger of one hand into the edge and, using the thumb and forefinger of the other hand, pinch the pastry. Continue all round the pastry edge.

8 Press together the pastry trimmings and roll out again. Cut out mushroom shapes with a sharp knife and stick them on to the pastry lid with beaten egg. Glaze the lid with beaten egg and cut several slits in the pastry to allow the steam to escape.

9 Bake the pie for about 30 minutes, until the pastry has browned. Serve the pie hot.

Nutritional information per portion: Energy 576kcal/2403kJ; Protein 23.8g; Carbohydrate 39.6g, of which sugars 4.7g; Fat 36.9g, of which saturates 20.3g; Cholesterol 127mg; Calcium 104mg; Fibre 3.1g; Sodium 334mg.

Lemon grass and coconut rice with green chicken curry

Use one or two fresh green chillies in this dish, according to how hot you like your curry. The mild aromatic flavour of the rice offsets the spiciness of the curry.

SERVES 3–4

4 spring onions (scallions), trimmed and
   roughly chopped
1–2 fresh green chillies, seeded and
   roughly chopped
2cm/³⁄₄in piece of fresh root
   ginger, peeled
2 garlic cloves
5ml/1 tsp Thai fish sauce
a large bunch of fresh coriander (cilantro)
a small handful of fresh parsley
30–45ml/2–3 tbsp water
30ml/2 tbsp sunflower oil
4 skinless, boneless chicken
   breasts, cubed

1 green (bell) pepper, seeded and
   finely sliced
200ml/7fl oz/scant 1 cup coconut milk
salt and ground black pepper

FOR THE RICE

225g/8oz/generous 1 cup Thai fragrant
   rice, rinsed
7200ml/7fl oz/scant 1 cup water
1 lemon grass stalk, quartered
   and bruised

1 Put the spring onions, chillies, ginger, garlic, fish sauce and fresh herbs in a food processor or blender. Pour in enough water to process to a smooth paste.

2 Heat half the oil in a large frying pan. Fry the chicken cubes until evenly browned. Transfer the chicken cubes to a plate.

3 Heat the remaining oil in the pan. Add the sliced green pepper and stir-fry for about 3–4 minutes, then add the chilli and ginger paste. Continue to fry, stirring, for about 3–4 minutes until the mixture becomes fairly thick.

4 Return the chicken to the pan and add the coconut milk and water. Season with salt and pepper and bring to the boil, then lower the heat. Half-cover the pan and simmer the contents for 8–10 minutes, until the chicken is completely cooked.

5 Using a slotted spoon, transfer the chicken and the green pepper mixture to a serving plate. Return the cooking liquid remaining in the pan to the heat and boil it for 10–12 minutes until it is well reduced and fairly thick.

6 Meanwhile, put the rice in a large pan. Add the coconut milk, water and bruised pieces of lemon grass. Stir in a little salt, bring to the boil, then lower the heat, cover and simmer very gently for 10 minutes, or for the time recommended on the packet. When the rice is tender, discard the pieces of lemon grass and fork the rice on to a warmed serving plate.

7 Return the chicken and peppers to the green curry sauce, stir well and cook gently for a few minutes to heat through. Spoon the curry over the rice, and serve immediately.

Nutritional information per portion: Energy 682kcal/2843kJ; Protein 43.4g; Carbohydrate 51g, of which sugars 5.9g; Fat 33.6g, of which saturates 23.4g; Cholesterol 105mg; Calcium 59mg; Fibre 1.5g; Sodium 108mg.

Roast chicken with baked potatoes and roasted garlic

Nothing beats a really good roast chicken. Rubbing the outside of the bird with lemon, smearing it generously with butter and sprinkling with salt will give a deep brown, crisp skin, and keep the flesh moist and succulent. The garlic roasts to a nutty melting softness.

SERVES 4

1.6kg/3^1/$_2$lb chicken
1 lemon
2 bay leaves
a small bunch of fresh thyme
50g/2oz/^{1}/$_4$ cup butter
salt and ground black pepper

FOR THE CREAMY BAKED POTATOES
50g/2oz/^{1}/$_4$ cup butter
900g/2lb waxy potatoes, such as Désirée or
   russet, peeled and thinly sliced

115g/4oz/1^1/$_3$ cups freshly grated Parmesan
   cheese
freshly grated nutmeg
1 egg, beaten
300ml/^{1}/$_2$ pint/1^1/$_4$ cups double (heavy)
   cream
salt and ground black pepper

FOR THE ROASTED GARLIC
4–6 garlic bulbs

1 Preheat the oven to 160°C/325°F/Gas 3. To make the baked potatoes, butter a shallow, flameproof dish. Layer the potatoes in the dish, sprinkling each layer with some of the cheese, nutmeg, and salt and pepper. Désirée potatoes have a lovely creamy texture, and will stick together nicely during cooking, whereas floury potatoes only disintegrate into mush.

2 Beat the egg and cream together, and pour it over the potatoes. Sprinkle any remaining cheese over the top.

3 Put the dish on top of the stove and lightly warm it through before baking in the oven for about 1 hour, or until the potatoes are tender and the top is golden and crisp. (This dish reheats very well, so it is worth making before you roast the chicken to make sure it is perfectly cooked.) Remove from the oven. Turn the oven up to 200°C/400°F/Gas 6.

4 Untie any trussing and tuck the wings under the chicken. Remove any fat from the cavity. Cut the lemon in half and rub the cut halves all over the chicken. Tuck the lemon halves inside the cavity along with the herbs. Spread the butter all over the breast and legs, seasoning well. Put the bird in a roasting pan.

5 Peel away some of the papery skin from the garlic bulbs. Ease each one apart, but make sure the cloves are still attached. Sit them on a double sheet of kitchen foil and bring the foil up to form a parcel. Pour in 45ml/3 tbsp water and close the parcel. Seal and put in the oven with the chicken.

6 After 45 minutes, remove the roasting pan from the oven, lift out and open the bag of garlic and set it on a baking dish. Return the chicken to the oven and cook for another 15 minutes, or until starting to go brown. Test the chicken to see if it is cooked, by inserting a skewer into the thickest part of the thigh. If the juices run clear, it is cooked, but if they are still pink, cook for another 10–15 minutes. Allow the bird to rest in the turned off oven for 15 minutes before carving.

7 Remove the chicken from the oven and pour out any juices caught in the cavity into the pan. Serve the chicken with the cooking juices, the roasted garlic and the creamy baked potatoes.

Nutritional information per portion: Energy 1142kcal/4768kJ; Protein 59g; Carbohydrate 43g, of which sugars 3g; Fat 83g, of which saturates 47g; Cholesterol 400mg; Calcium 391mg; Fibre 3.6g; Sodium 626mg.

Chinese fried rice

This dish is a variation of egg fried rice. It is quick, simple and inexpensive to prepare; most importantly, it is also extremely tasty and satisfying. Enjoy it with a bottle of wine.

SERVES 4

50g/1³/₄oz cooked ham
50g/1³/₄oz cooked prawns
   (shrimp), peeled
3 eggs
5ml/1 tsp salt
2 spring onions (scallions), finely chopped
60ml/4 tbsp vegetable oil
115g/4oz/1 cup peas, thawed if frozen
15ml/1 tbsp light soy sauce
15ml/1 tbsp Chinese rice wine or
   dry sherry
450g/1lb/4 cups cooked white long
   grain rice

1 Dice the cooked ham finely. Pat the cooked prawns dry on kitchen paper.

2 In a bowl, beat the eggs lightly with a pinch of the salt and a few pieces of the spring onions.

3 Heat about half the oil in a wok, stir-fry the peas, prawns and ham for 1 minute, then add the soy sauce, and rice wine or sherry. Transfer to a bowl and keep hot.

4 Heat the remaining oil in the wok and scramble the eggs lightly. Add the rice and stir to make sure that the grains are separate. Add the remaining salt, the remaining spring onions and the prawn mixture. Toss over the heat to mix, and heat through, if serving hot. Serve hot or cold.

Nutritional information per portion: Energy 86kcal/360kJ; Protein 9.8g; Carbohydrate 3.8g, of which sugars 1.2g; Fat 3.7g, of which saturates 1g; Cholesterol 127mg; Calcium 34mg; Fibre 1.4g; Sodium 477mg.

Spaghetti with minced beef sauce

This recipe brings back happy memories of flat-sharing and communal eating. Any bolognaise leftovers will taste even better the next day and the sauce freezes well.

SERVES 4–6

30ml/2 tbsp olive oil
1 onion, finely chopped
1 garlic clove, crushed
5ml/1 tsp dried mixed herbs
1.25ml/¼ tsp cayenne pepper
350–450g/12oz–1lb minced (ground) beef
400g/14oz can chopped plum tomatoes
45ml/3 tbsp tomato ketchup
15ml/1 tbsp sun-dried tomato paste
5ml/1 tsp Worcestershire sauce
5ml/1 tsp dried oregano
450ml/¾ pint/1¾ cups beef or
    vegetable stock
45ml/3 tbsp red wine
400–450g/14oz–1lb dried spaghetti
salt and ground black pepper
freshly grated Parmesan cheese, to serve

1 Heat the oil in a medium pan, add the onion and garlic and cook gently, stirring often, for 5 minutes until softened. Stir in the mixed herbs and cayenne and cook for 2–3 minutes. Add the minced beef and cook gently for 5 minutes, stirring often, breaking up any lumps with a wooden spoon.

2 Stir in the canned tomatoes, ketchup, sun-dried tomato paste, Worcestershire sauce, oregano and plenty of black pepper. Pour in the stock and red wine and bring to the boil, stirring. Cover the pan, lower the heat and leave the sauce to simmer for 30 minutes, stirring occasionally.

3 Cook the pasta according to the instructions on the packet. Drain well and divide among warmed bowls. Taste the sauce and add a little salt if necessary, then spoon it on top of the pasta and sprinkle with a little grated Parmesan. Serve immediately, with grated Parmesan handed around separately.

Nutritional information per portion: Energy 396kcal/1682kJ; Protein 30.2g; Carbohydrate 62.3g, of which sugars 8.8g; Fat 2.8g, of which saturates 0.6g; Cholesterol 43mg; Calcium 43mg; Fibre 4.8g; Sodium 82mg.

Lasagne

This is the classic lasagne al forno. It is based on a rich, meaty filling, as you would expect from an authentic Bolognese recipe. Make it the day before and on all you need to do the next evening is pop it in the oven and relax with an aperitif while it cooks.

SERVES 6

12 "no-need-to-pre-cook" dried lasagne
   sheets
50g/2oz/²⁄₃ cup freshly grated Parmesan
   cheese
100ml/3¹⁄₂fl oz/scant ¹⁄₂ cup double
   (heavy) cream

**FOR THE BOLOGNESE MEAT
SAUCE**
25g/1oz/2 tbsp butter
15ml/1 tbsp olive oil
1 onion, chopped
2 carrots, sliced
2 celery sticks, chopped
2 garlic cloves, chopped

130g/4¹⁄₂oz pancetta or rindless streaky
   (fatty) bacon, diced
250g/9oz lean minced (ground) beef
250g/9oz lean minced (ground) pork
120ml/4fl oz/¹⁄₂ cup dry white wine
2 x 400g/14oz cans crushed Italian plum
   tomatoes
475–750ml/16fl oz–1¹⁄₄ pints/2–3 cups beef
   stock, plus 150–250ml/5–8fl oz/²⁄₃–1 cup
   extra if required

FOR THE WHITE SAUCE
50g/2oz/¹⁄₄ cup butter
50g/2oz/¹⁄₂ cup plain (all-purpose) flour
900ml/1¹⁄₂ pints/3³⁄₄ cups hot milk
salt and ground black pepper

1 If you are making the Bolognese sauce, heat the butter and oil in a large skillet or pan until sizzling. Add the vegetables, garlic, and the pancetta or bacon and cook over a medium heat, stirring frequently, for 20 minutes or until the vegetables have softened.

2 Add the minced beef and pork, lower the heat and cook gently for 10 minutes, stirring frequently and breaking up any lumps in the meat with a wooden spoon. Stir in salt and pepper to taste, then add the wine and canned tomatoes and stir again. Simmer for about 5 minutes, or until reduced.

3 Preheat the oven to 190°C/375°F/Gas 5. If the Bolognese is cold, reheat it. Once hot, stir in enough additional beef stock to make it quite runny.

4 Make the white sauce. Melt the butter in a medium pan, add the flour and cook, stirring, for 1–2 minutes. Add the milk a little at a time, whisking vigorously after each addition. Bring to the boil and cook, stirring, until the sauce is smooth and thick. Add salt and pepper to taste, whisk well to mix, then remove from the heat.

5 Spread about a third of the Bolognese sauce over the bottom of a baking dish.

6 Cover the Bolognese sauce in the bottom of the dish with about a quarter of the white sauce, followed by four sheets of lasagne. Repeat the layers twice more, then cover the top layer of lasagne with the remaining white sauce and sprinkle the grated Parmesan evenly over the top.

7 Bake for 40–45 minutes or until the pasta feels tender when pierced with a skewer. Allow to stand for about 10 minutes before serving.

Nutritional information per portion: Energy 472kcal/1994kJ; Protein 20.5g; Carbohydrate 66g, of which sugars 10.4g; Fat 16g, of which saturates 8.8g; Cholesterol 43mg; Calcium 316mg; Fibre 2g; Sodium 296mg.

Stewed lamb in a creamy dill sauce

This good, old-fashioned lamb dish is made with onion, carrot and celery. The ideal accompaniment is boiled new potatoes drizzled with butter.

SERVES 6–8

1kg/2¼lb lamb neck fillet or boned leg, cubed

1 Spanish (Bermuda) onion, chopped

1 carrot, chopped

1 celery stick, chopped

1 bay leaf

2 sprigs fresh thyme

FOR THE SAUCE

a bunch of fresh dill

250ml/8fl oz/1 cup water

90g/3½oz/½ cup sugar

120ml/4fl oz/½ cup white vinegar

10g/¼oz/½ tbsp butter, softened

10g/¼oz/½ tbsp plain (all-purpose) flour

1 egg yolk

120ml/4fl oz/½ cup double (heavy) cream

salt and ground black pepper

1 Put the lamb in a pan and add the other main ingredients. Cover with cold water, bring to simmering point and simmer for 40 minutes to 1 hour.

2 Remove the dill fronds from the main stalks, chop and set aside. Put the reserved stalks in a pan and add the water, sugar and vinegar. Bring to the boil and boil for 5 minutes.

3 Put the butter in a bowl and work in the flour with a fork to make a beurre manié. Mix the egg yolk and cream together.

4 When the lamb is cooked, put 1 litre/1¾ pints/4 cups of the lamb stock in a pan. Strain in the sugar and vinegar liquid and bring to simmering point.

5 Add small knobs (pats) of the beurre manié, whisking, allowing each to melt before adding another, to thicken the sauce. Bring to the boil and simmer for 10 minutes.

6 Stir the egg and cream and the dill fronds into the sauce. Don't allow to boil. Serve the sauce with the lamb.

Nutritional information per portion: Energy 509kcal/2125kJ; Protein 34.4g; Carbohydrate 22.6g, of which sugars 20.1g; Fat 31.8g, of which saturates 16g; Cholesterol 191mg; Calcium 56mg; Fibre 1.2g; Sodium 169mg.

Meatballs in tomato sauce

Cook meatballs in their sauce, rather than frying them first, because this helps keep them nice and moist. Serve in the traditional way with spaghetti and shavings of Parmesan cheese.

SERVES 4

225g/8oz/1 cup minced (ground) beef
4 Sicilian-style sausages
**2 x 400g/14oz cans pomodorino
    tomatoes**
salt and ground black pepper
**spaghetti and Parmesan cheese, shaved,
    to serve**

1 Put the minced beef in a bowl and season with salt and pepper. Remove the sausages from their skins and mix them thoroughly into the beef.

2 Shape the mixture into balls about the size of large walnuts and arrange in a single layer in a shallow baking dish. Cover and chill for 30 minutes.

3 Preheat the oven to 180°C/350°F/Gas 4. Process the tomatoes in a food processor or blender until just smooth, and season. Pour over the meatballs, making sure they are all covered.

4 Bake the meatballs for 40 minutes, stirring once or twice until they are cooked through, then serve.

Nutritional information per portion meatballs: Energy 309kcal/1290kJ; Protein 22g; Carbohydrate 12g, of which sugars 7g; Fat 20g, of which saturates 8g; Cholesterol 70mg; Calcium 80mg; Fibre 2g; Sodium 800mg.

Steak and mushroom pudding

This pudding has a suet crust and is a glorious recipe to cook for a special occasion. Here it is filled with lean beef, dried porcini and fresh mushrooms, and the suet crust is scented heavily with lemon and herbs, especially thyme. While it steams away, the aroma is amazing.

SERVES 6

25g/1oz/$\frac{1}{2}$ cup dried porcini mushrooms, soaked in warm water for 20 minutes
1.3kg/3lb rump (round) steak, trimmed
30ml/2 tbsp plain (all-purpose) flour
30ml/2 tbsp olive or sunflower oil
1 large onion, chopped
225g/8oz chestnut or open cup mushrooms, halved or quartered if large
300ml/$\frac{1}{2}$ pint/1$\frac{1}{4}$ cups fruity red wine
300ml/$\frac{1}{2}$ pint/1$\frac{1}{4}$ cups beef stock
45ml/3 tbsp mushroom ketchup (optional)
1 bay leaf
salt and ground black pepper

FOR THE HERBY SUET CRUST

275g/10oz/2$\frac{1}{2}$ cups self-raising (self-rising) flour
5ml/1 tsp baking powder
15ml/1 tbsp each finely chopped fresh parsley, sage, rosemary and thyme
finely grated rind of 1 lemon
75g/3oz/1$\frac{1}{2}$ cups beef or vegetable suet
50g/2oz/$\frac{1}{4}$ cup butter, chilled and grated
1 egg, beaten
juice of $\frac{1}{2}$ lemon
150ml/$\frac{1}{4}$ pint/$\frac{2}{3}$ cup cold water

1 Preheat the oven to 180°C/350°F/Gas 4. Drain the porcini mushrooms, reserving the soaking liquid, and roughly chop. Cut the steak into large cubes, then toss the steak with the flour and plenty of salt and pepper.

2 Heat the oil in a large, heavy frying pan until very hot. Add the onion and cook, stirring frequently, until golden brown. Using a slotted spoon, transfer the onion to an ovenproof casserole. Fry the floured steak in batches until well browned on all sides.

3 Add the meat to the casserole with the chopped porcini and the fresh mushrooms and stir well. Pour in the reserved soaking liquid, wine and stock, add the mushroom ketchup, if using, and tuck in the bay leaf. Cover and cook in the oven for 1$\frac{1}{2}$ hours, until the meat is tender. Allow the mixture to cool completely.

4 To make the herby suet crust, butter a deep 1.7 litre/3 pint/7 cup heatproof bowl. Sift the flour, baking powder and 2.5ml/$\frac{1}{2}$ tsp salt into a large mixing bowl.

5 Stir the herbs and lemon rind into the flour mixture and season with plenty of pepper. Stir in the suet and butter. Make a well in the centre, add the egg, lemon juice and enough of the cold water to mix and gather into a soft but manageable dough.

6 Knead the dough lightly on a well-floured work surface. Cut off a quarter of the dough and wrap in clear film (plastic wrap). Shape the rest into a ball and roll out into a large round, big enough to line the heatproof bowl. Lift up the dough and drop it into the bowl, pressing against the sides to line the bowl evenly. Roll out the reserved pastry to a round large enough to use as a lid.

7 Spoon in the beef filling to within 1cm/½in of the rim. Top up with the gravy. (Keep the remaining gravy to serve with the pudding later.) Dampen the edges of the pastry and fit the lid. Press the edges to seal and trim away the excess pastry.

8 Cover the bowl with pleated, buttered baking parchment, then with pleated foil to allow for the crust to rise. Tie string under the lip of the bowl to hold the paper in place, then take it over the top to form a handle. Place the bowl in a large pan of simmering water, cover and steam for 1½ hours, topping up with boiling water as necessary. Bring the bowl to the table wrapped in a clean dish towel and serve the pudding straight from the bowl.

Nutritional information per portion: Energy 637kcal/2652kJ; Protein 18.7g; Carbohydrate 46.2g, of which sugars 5.2g; Fat 43.4g, of which saturates 13.1g; Cholesterol 259mg; Calcium 99mg; Fibre 4.4g; Sodium 941mg.

Lamb shanks and apricots with couscous

Traditionally called a tagine, this dish is simply a stew that has been simmered on the stove for a long time. It is perfect when you are catering for a crowd, as you just leave it to cook.

SERVES 6

50g/2oz/¼ cup butter
6 lamb shanks
1 onion, finely chopped
2.5ml/½ tsp ground cumin
2.5ml/½ tsp ground ginger
2.5ml/½ tsp ground cinnamon
10ml/2 tsp paprika
4 cloves
115g/4oz/1 cup ground almonds
3 large strips orange rind
225g/8oz/1 cup dried apricots

115g/4oz/½ cup stoned (pitted) prunes
115g/4oz/scant 1 cup muscatel raisins
30ml/2 tbsp orange flower water (optional)
salt and ground black pepper

FOR THE MINTED SESAME COUSCOUS
375g/13oz quick-cook couscous
115g/4oz/½ cup butter, cubed
60ml/4 tbsp chopped fresh mint
45ml/3 tbsp sesame seeds

1 Melt the butter in a large pan. Brown the lamb shanks, three at a time, and transfer to a plate. Stir the onion and spices into the pan juices and cook for 5 minutes. Add 2.5ml/½ tsp each salt and pepper. Stir in the almonds.

2 Return the lamb to the pan with the orange rind and cover with 1.2 litres/2 pints/5 cups water. Bring to the boil, then turn the heat to very low. Cover the surface of the stew with a sheet of crumpled baking parchment, then the lid. Simmer for 1 hour.

3 After this time, add the apricots, prunes and raisins, stir them in and simmer for an hour. Just before serving, put the couscous into a measuring jug (cup) and note the measurement. Transfer to a bowl and measure out twice its volume in boiling water. Stir the butter and mint into the boiling water, then pour over the couscous. Cover tightly with clear film (plastic wrap) and leave for 5 minutes.

4 Toast the sesame seeds in a pan until golden brown. Uncover the couscous and fluff up the grains with a fork. Add the sesame seeds, taste and season. Taste the lamb for seasoning and add the orange flower water, if using. Serve with the couscous.

Nutritional information per portion: Energy 565kcal/2368kJ; Protein 36.3g; Carbohydrate 60g, of which sugars 35.2g; Fat 21.6g, of which saturates 8.6g; Cholesterol 119mg; Calcium 143mg; Fibre 6g; Sodium 203mg.

Beef, beetroot and potato gratin

This variation of an unusual Polish mix of flavours produces a very hearty main meal. Horseradish and mustard are great with both the beef and the beetroot, most of which is hidden underneath making a colourful surprise when you serve it.

SERVES 4

30ml/2 tbsp vegetable oil

1 small onion, chopped

15ml/1 tbsp plain (all-purpose) flour

150ml/¼ pint/⅔ cup vegetable stock

225g/8oz cooked beetroot (beet), drained
    well and chopped

15ml/1 tbsp creamed horseradish

15ml/1 tbsp caraway seeds

3 shallots, or 1 medium onion, chopped

450g/1lb frying or grilling steak, cut into thin
    strips

225g/8oz assorted mushrooms, sliced

10–15ml/2–3 tsp hot mustard

60ml/4 tbsp sour cream

45ml/3 tbsp chopped fresh parsley

salt and ground black pepper

FOR THE POTATO BORDER

900g/2lb floury potatoes

150ml/¼ pint/⅔ cup milk

25g/1oz/2 tbsp butter

15ml/1 tbsp chopped fresh dill (optional)

1 Preheat the oven to 190°C/375°F/Gas 5. Lightly oil a baking or gratin dish. Heat 15ml/1 tbsp of the vegetable oil in a large pan, add the onion and fry until softened but not coloured.

2 Stir in the flour, remove the pan from the heat and gradually add the stock, stirring constantly until well blended and smooth.

3 Return the pan to the heat and simmer until thickened, stirring all the while. Add the beetroot (but reserve a few pieces for the topping, if you wish), horseradish and caraway seeds. Mix gently, then put to one side.

4 To make the potato border, first cook the potatoes in a large pan with plenty of boiling salted water for 20 minutes until the potatoes are tender. Drain the potatoes well through a colander and mash well with the milk and butter. Add the chopped dill, if using, and season the mixture with salt and pepper to taste. Stir to combine the seasonings.

5 Spoon the potatoes into the prepared dish and push them well up the sides, making a large hollow in the middle for the filling. Spoon the beetroot mixture into the well, evening it out with the back of a spoon, and set aside.

6 Heat the remaining oil in a large frying pan, add the shallots or onion and fry until softened but not coloured. Add the steak and stir-fry quickly until browned all over. Then add the mushrooms and fry quickly until most of their juices have cooked away. Remove the pan from the heat and gently stir in the mustard, sour cream, seasoning to taste and half the parsley until well blended.

7 Spoon the steak mixture over the beetroot mixture in the baking dish, sprinkling the reserved beetroot over the top, cover and bake for around 30 minutes. Serve hot, sprinkled with the remaining parsley.

COOK'S TIP
If planning ahead, for instance for a dinner party, this entire dish can be made in advance and heated through when needed. Allow 50 minutes baking time from room temperature. Add the beetroot pieces to the topping near the end of the cooking time.

Nutritional information per portion: Energy 560kcal/2346kJ; Protein 34.1g; Carbohydrate 49.5g, of which sugars 12g; Fat 26.4g, of which saturates 10.8g; Cholesterol 91mg; Calcium 111mg; Fibre 4.6g; Sodium 354mg.

Moussaka

This classic Greek dish with layers of lamb, potatoes and aubergines has a rich cheesy topping and makes a substantial meal. It takes time to prepare but can be made in advance.

SERVES 6

30ml/2 tbsp olive oil
30ml/2 tbsp chopped fresh oregano
1 large onion, finely chopped
675g/1½lb lean lamb, minced (ground)
1 large aubergine (eggplant), sliced
2 x 400g/14oz cans chopped tomatoes
45ml/3 tbsp tomato purée (paste)

1 lamb stock cube
2 floury potatoes, halved
115g/4oz/1 cup Cheddar cheese, grated
150ml/¼ pint/⅔ cup single (light) cream
salt and ground black pepper
fresh bread, to serve

1 Preheat the oven to 180°C/350°F/Gas 4. Heat the olive oil in a large deep-sided frying pan. Fry the oregano and onion over a low heat, stirring frequently, for about 5 minutes or until the onion has softened.

2 Stir in the lamb and cook for 10 minutes until browned. Grill (broil) the aubergine slices on a high heat for 5 minutes until browned, turning once.

3 Stir the tomatoes and purée into the meat mixture, crumble the stock cube over it, stir well, season and simmer uncovered for a further 15 minutes.

4 Cook the potatoes in lightly salted boiling water for 5–10 minutes until just tender. Drain, and when cool enough to handle, cut into thin slices.

5 Layer the aubergines, meat and potatoes in a 1.75 litre/3 pint/7½ cup oval ovenproof dish, finishing with a layer of potatoes.

6 Mix the cheese and cream together in a bowl and pour over the top of the other ingredients in the dish. Cook for 45–50 minutes until bubbling and golden on the top. Serve straight from the dish, while hot, with plenty of fresh, crusty bread.

Nutritional information per portion: Energy 588kcal/2444kJ; Protein 37.9g; Carbohydrate 14.8g, of which sugars 3.7g; Fat 40.9g, of which saturates 18.2g; Cholesterol 206mg; Calcium 379mg; Fibre 2.4g; Sodium 506mg.

Sausages, mustard, mashed potato and onion gravy

This scrumptious dish will bring sunshine to any grey day. Long, slow cooking is important for good onion gravy as this reduces and caramelizes the onions to create a sweet flavour.

SERVES 4

12 pork and leek sausages
salt and ground black pepper

FOR THE ONION GRAVY
30ml/2 tbsp olive oil
25g/1oz/2 tbsp butter
8 onions, sliced
5ml/1 tsp caster (superfine) sugar
15ml/1 tbsp plain (all-purpose) flour
300ml/1/2 pint/11/4 cups beef stock

FOR THE MASHED POTATO
1.5kg/31/4lb floury potatoes
50g/2oz/1/4 cup butter
150ml/1/4 pint/2/3 cup double (heavy)
  cream
15ml/1 tbsp wholegrain mustard

1 Heat the oil and butter in a large pan. Add the onions and stir. Cover and cook for 30 minutes on a low heat. Add the sugar and cook for 5 minutes, until the onions are soft.

2 Remove the pan from the heat, stir in the flour, then the stock. Return to the heat. Bring to the boil, stirring, then simmer until thickened. Season.

3 Cook the potatoes in boiling salted water for 20 minutes, or until tender.

4 Drain the potatoes and mash them with the butter, cream and wholegrain mustard. Season.

5 While the potatoes are cooking, preheat the grill (broiler) to medium. Arrange the sausages in a single layer in the grill (broiling) pan and cook for 15–20 minutes, or until cooked, turning frequently so that they brown evenly.

6 Serve the sausages with the mashed potato and onion gravy.

Nutritional information per portion: Energy 1425kcal/5921kJ; Protein 31.4g; Carbohydrate 106.1g, of which sugars 22.3g; Fat 100.3g, of which saturates 45.1g; Cholesterol 176mg; Calcium 190mg; Fibre 10g; Sodium 1634mg.

Pork sausage stew

This hearty casserole, made with spicy sausages and haricot beans, is flavoured with fragrant fresh herbs and dry wine. Serve with crusty bread for mopping up the delicious juices.

SERVES 4

225g/8oz/1¼ cups dried haricot (navy) beans
2 sprigs fresh thyme
30ml/2 tbsp olive oil
450g/1lb fresh pork sausages
1 onion, finely chopped
2 sticks celery, finely diced
300ml/½ pint/1¼ cups dry white wine
a sprig of fresh rosemary
1 bay leaf
300ml/½ pint/1¼ cups boiling vegetable stock
200g/7oz can chopped tomatoes
¼ head dark green cabbage, shredded
salt and ground black pepper
chopped fresh thyme, to garnish
crusty bread, to serve

1 Put the haricot beans in a bowl and cover with cold water. Soak for at least 8 hours, or overnight.

2 Drain the beans and put in a pan with the thyme and cold water to cover. Bring to the boil and boil for 10 minutes, then drain and return to the pan, discarding the thyme.

3 Heat the oil in a frying pan and cook the sausages until brown. Add to the beans and discard all but 15ml/1 tbsp of the fat in the pan.

4 Add the onion and celery to the frying pan and cook for 5 minutes. Add the wine, rosemary and bay leaf and bring to the boil. Pour over the sausages, add the stock and seasoning. Cover and simmer very slowly for 5–6 hours.

5 Stir the tomatoes and the cabbage into the stew. Cover and cook for 30–45 minutes until the cabbage is tender. Divide between warmed plates, garnish with thyme and serve with crusty bread.

Nutritional information per portion: Energy 620kcal/2593kJ; Protein 28.4g; Carbohydrate 47.4g, of which sugars 9.9g; Fat 30.9g, of which saturates 10.8g; Cholesterol 67.5mg; Calcium 205mg; Fibre 7.6g; Sodium 1139mg.

Chill-out Desserts

If you need a bit of cheering up then be grateful for the excuse to indulge in an irresistible sweet. Here are a fabulous selection of chilled desserts, including Rippled Nectarine and Muscovado Terrine, Rhubarb and Ginger Trifles, Orange Crêpes with Mascarpone Cream and Baked Caramel Custard. Dishes such as these are also sublime cool-you-downs for garden gatherings in the heat of summer.

Classic vanilla ice cream

Nothing beats the creamy simplicity of true vanilla ice cream. And once you've tried this luxurious home-made version, there really is no going back.

SERVES 4

1 vanilla pod (bean)
300ml/¹⁄₂ pint/1¹⁄₄ cups semi-skimmed (low-fat) milk
4 egg yolks
75g/3oz/6 tbsp caster (superfine) sugar
5ml/1 tsp cornflour (cornstarch)
300ml/¹⁄₂ pint/1¹⁄₄ cups double (heavy) cream

1 Slit the vanilla pod lengthways. Pour the milk into a heavy pan, add the vanilla pod and bring to the boil. Remove from the heat and leave for 15 minutes.

2 Hold the pod over the pan and, with a small knife, scrape the seeds into the milk. Return the pan to the heat and bring back to the boil.

3 Whisk the egg yolks, sugar and cornflour in a bowl until thick and foamy. Gradually pour on the hot milk, whisking constantly. Return the mixture to the pan and cook over a gentle heat, stirring all the time.

4 When the custard thickens and is smooth, pour it back into the bowl. Cool it, then chill.

5 Whip the cream until it has thickened but still falls from a spoon. Fold it into the custard and pour into a plastic tub or similar freezerproof container.

6 Freeze for 6 hours or until firm enough to scoop, beating twice with a fork, or in a food processor.

7 Scoop into dishes, bowls or bought cones – or eat straight from the tub.

Nutritional information per portion: Energy 546kcal/2264kJ; Protein 6.8g; Carbohydrate 25.6g, of which sugars 24.4g; Fat 47.1g, of which saturates 27.4g; Cholesterol 309mg; Calcium 160mg; Fibre 0g; Sodium 60mg.

Rippled nectarine and muscovado terrine

This sumptuous combination of nectarine ice cream, cream cheese and brown sugar is set in the corner of a tilted square cake tin to create an interesting triangular shape.

SERVES 6–8

50g/2oz/¼ cup light muscovado (brown) sugar
7.5ml/1½ tsp hot water
200g/7oz/scant 1 cup cream cheese
115g/4oz/1 cup icing (confectioners') sugar
90ml/6 tbsp full cream (whole) milk
3 ripe nectarines
10ml/2 tsp lemon juice
100ml/3½ fl oz/scant ½ cup extra thick double (heavy) cream

1 Line one half of a 20cm/8in square cake tin (pan) with clear film (plastic wrap). Dissolve the sugar in the water, stirring to form a syrup. Beat the cream cheese in a bowl with a quarter of the icing sugar until soft and smooth; then beat in the milk.

2 Halve and stone (pit) the nectarines and purée with the lemon juice and remaining icing sugar.

3 Whip the cream, then fold in the purée. Prop the tin at a 45° angle. Spoon in a third of the nectarine purée. Place spoonfuls of the cream cheese mixture over the purée.

4 Drizzle with half the muscovado syrup. Spoon half the remaining nectarine mixture into the tin, then spoon over the remaining cream cheese, syrup and nectarine mixture.

5 Using a dessertspoon handle, fold the mixtures together in about six strokes to lightly ripple the ingredients. Freeze overnight, keeping the tin propped at a 45° angle in the freezer; then lay flat.

6 Transfer to the refridgerator 30 minutes before serving to soften. Turn out on a serving plate and peel away the film. Serve in slices.

Nutritional information per portion: Energy 495kcal/2060kJ; Protein 2.6g; Carbohydrate 38.9g, of which sugars 38.7g; Fat 33.9g, of which saturates 20.9g; Cholesterol 70mg; Calcium 47mg; Fibre 1.7g; Sodium 16mg.

Crumbled chocolate brownie ice cream

This is the most wickedly indulgent dessert. The only risk is getting stuck into the rich brownies before you make the ice cream. There are many brownie recipes, but this one is sublime.

SERVES 6

1.2 litres/2 pints/5 cups good quality
   chocolate or chocolate chip ice cream

FOR THE CHOCOLATE BROWNIES
75g/3oz dark (bittersweet) chocolate with
   70% cocoa solids
115g/4oz/½ cup butter, plus extra for
   greasing
4 eggs, beaten

10ml/2 tsp vanilla extract
400g/14oz/2 cups caster (superfine)
   sugar
115g/4oz/1 cup plain (all-purpose) flour
25g/1oz/¼ cup unsweetened cocoa powder
115g/4oz dark (bittersweet) chocolate chips
115g/4oz/1 cup chopped walnuts

1 First make the chocolate brownies. Preheat the oven to 190°C/375°F/ Gas 5. Liberally butter an 18 x 28cm/7 x 11in shallow baking tin (pan) and line the base with baking parchment.

2 Break up the chocolate into pieces and put it in a bowl with the butter. Place the bowl over a pan of barely simmering water and leave until the contents have melted. Remove the bowl from the heat and stir in the beaten eggs, vanilla and sugar. Mix well together.

3 Sift the flour with the cocoa powder and beat into the chocolate mixture. Gently stir in the chocolate chips and walnuts.

4 Pour the mixture into the tin and level the surface. Bake for about 35 minutes. To test if the brownies are fully cooked, insert a metal skewer in the centre – it is ready if it comes out clean. The cake should be set but still moist. (Overcooking will make the brownies dry.) When completely cold, cut into squares or bars.

5 To make the chocolate brownie ice cream, cut about 175g/6oz of the brownies into small cubes. Soften the ice cream and lightly stir in the chopped brownies. Spoon the mixture into a large freezerproof container, cover and freeze for at least 2 hours before serving.

Nutritional information per portion: Energy 1255kcal/5248kJ; Protein 19.4g; Carbohydrate 139.4g, of which sugars 123.7g; Fat 72.8g, of which saturates 36.1g; Cholesterol 170mg; Calcium 319mg; Fibre 2.6g; Sodium 330mg.

Red fruit compote

This is a magically simple but very elegant dessert. During the summer this can be made with fresh berries, but you can also use any combination of frozen fruit.

SERVES 4

20g/³⁄₄oz caster (superfine) sugar
200ml/7fl oz/scant 1 cup red grape juice
2 pieces of star anise
1 cinnamon stick
15g/¹⁄₂oz/2 tbsp cornflour (cornstarch)
450g/1lb mixed berries (strawberries,
blueberries, cranberries, blackberries,
raspberries or redcurrants), washed
fresh mint leaves, to decorate
single (light) cream, to serve

1 Heat the sugar in a pan over medium heat until it caramelizes. When it turns golden brown, plunge the base of the pan in a bowl of cold water to stop the sugar burning.

2 Stir in the grape juice, add the spices and return to the heat.

3 Mix the cornflour with a little cold water.

4 When the juice comes to the boil, stir in the cornflour mixture and cook, stirring, for 1 minute.

5 Halve any large berries, and add them to the hot juice, bring to the boil again, then remove from the heat and leave to cool. Spoon the cold compote into bowls, decorate with mint leaves and serve with cream.

Nutritional information per portion: Energy 86kcal/366kJ; Protein 1.1g; Carbohydrate 21.3g, of which sugars 17.8g; Fat 0.2g, of which saturates 0g; Cholesterol 0mg; Calcium 31mg; Fibre 1.3g; Sodium 13mg

Rhubarb and ginger trifles

There are only three ingredients in this recipe, so it couldn't be simpler. Make sure you choose a good quality jar of rhubarb compote; try to find one with large, chunky pieces of fruit.

SERVES 4

12 gingernut biscuits (gingersnaps)
50ml/2fl oz/¼ cup rhubarb compote
450ml/¾ pint/scant 2 cups extra thick
   double (heavy) cream

1 Put the ginger biscuits in a plastic bag and seal it. Bash the biscuits with a rolling pin until they are roughly crushed.

2 Set aside two tablespoons of crushed biscuits and divide the rest among four serving glasses.

3 Spoon the rhubarb compote on top of the crushed biscuits, then top with the cream. Chill for about 30 minutes, until needed.

4 Sprinkle the reserved crushed biscuits over the trifles and serve immediately.

Nutritional information per portion: Energy 695kcal/2874kJ; Protein 3.6g; Carbohydrate 27.1g, of which sugars 14.1g; Fat 64.3g, of which saturates 39.4g; Cholesterol 154mg; Calcium 98mg; Fibre 0.6g; Sodium 124mg.

Ice cream sundae with chocolate sauce

This immensely popular dessert consists of good quality vanilla ice cream lavishly drizzled with a decadent warm chocolate sauce. The topping is up to the individual, but whipped cream, chopped nuts, chocolate shavings, and a wafer can all be added. Make it at least a day ahead.

MAKES 10

350ml/12fl oz/1½ cups full cream (whole) milk
250ml/8fl oz/1 cup double (heavy) cream
1 vanilla pod (bean)
4 egg yolks
100g/3¾oz/½ cup caster (superfine) sugar
chopped nuts, chocolate curls and ice cream
   wafers, to serve (optional)

FOR THE CHOCOLATE SAUCE

60ml/4 tbsp double (heavy) cream
150ml/¼ pint/⅔ cup full cream (whole) milk
250g/9oz Callebaut callets (semisweet bits) or
   other good-quality chocolate, cut into small
   pieces
15ml/1 tbsp brandy or liqueur,
   such as Grand Marnier (optional)

1 First make the ice cream. Pour 250ml/8fl oz/1 cup of the milk into a heavy pan. Add the cream. Slit the vanilla pod down its length, scrape the seeds into the pan with the tip of the knife, then heat the mixture. When it is hot, but not boiling, remove it from the heat and leave to stand for 10 minutes.

2 Meanwhile, mix the egg yolks and sugar in a bowl and beat for 5 minutes, until thick and creamy. Still beating, add one-third of the warm milk mixture in a steady stream. Pour in the remaining milk mixture and whisk for 2 minutes.

3 Return the mixture to the pan and cook over medium-high heat, stirring constantly, for 5–7 minutes, until the custard is thick enough to coat the back of a spoon. Immediately remove the pan from the heat and stir in the remaining milk. Strain the custard into a stainless steel or glass bowl set over a bowl of iced water. When it has cooled to room temperature, cover and chill in the refrigerator.

4 Scrape the chilled mixture into a freezer container, cover and freeze until firm, whisking 2 or 3 times. Alternatively, use an ice cream maker, transferring the soft-serve ice cream to a tub and freezing it.

5 Make the chocolate sauce. Mix the cream and milk in a pan and heat to simmering point. Remove from the heat and stir in the chocolate pieces until they melt. Stir in the brandy or liqueur, if using. Pour 20ml/4 tsp of the warm chocolate sauce into each glass. Top with two scoops of ice cream and more of the sauce. Sprinkle with chopped nuts or chocolate curls, or top with a wafer, if you like.

Per portion Energy 930kcal/3869kJ; Protein 11.2g; Carbohydrate 72.3g, of which sugars 71.7g; Fat 68.2g, of which saturates 40.2g; Cholesterol 324mg; Calcium 229mg; Fibre 1.6g; Sodium 80mg.

Toasted marzipan parcels with plums

Melting ice cream in lightly toasted marzipan makes an irresistible dessert for anyone who likes the flavour of almonds. You can use apricots, cherries or pears instead of plums, if you prefer.

SERVES 4

400g/14oz golden marzipan
icing (confectioners') sugar, for dusting
250ml/8fl oz/1 cup Classic Vanilla
   Ice Cream (see page 152)

FOR THE PLUM COMPOTE
3 red plums, about 250g/9oz
25g/1oz/2 tbsp caster (superfine) sugar
75ml/5 tbsp water

1 Roll out the marzipan on a surface lightly dusted with sifted icing sugar to a 45 x 23cm/18 x 9in rectangle. Then stamp out eight rounds using a plain 12cm/4$^{1}/_{2}$in biscuit cutter.

2 Place a spoonful of the ice cream in the centre of one of the circles. Bring the marzipan up over the ice cream and press the edges together to completely encase.

3 Crimp the edges with your fingers. Transfer to a small baking sheet and freeze. Fill and shape the remaining parcels in the same way and then freeze overnight.

4 Halve and stone (pit) the plums. Heat the sugar and water in a heavy pan, stirring until the sugar has completely dissolved.

5 Add the plums and cook very gently until tender but holding their shape. Test with the tip of a knife.

6 Preheat the grill (broiler) to high. Cook the marzipan parcels on the rack for 1–2 minutes, watching closely, until the crimped edge of the marzipan is lightly browned. Transfer the parcels to serving plates and serve with the warm plum compote.

Nutritional information per portion: Energy 547kcal/2307kJ; Protein 8g; Carbohydrate 92g, of which sugars 91.3g; Fat 18.1g, of which saturates 4.9g; Cholesterol 15mg; Calcium 140mg; Fibre 2.9g; Sodium 59mg.

Orange crêpes with mascarpone cream

With this delicious recipe, which is neither too rich nor too sweet, the sorbet and mascarpone simply melt together in their crisp, delicate pancake cases.

SERVES 8

FOR THE CRÊPES
115g/4oz/1 cup plain (all-purpose) flour
300ml/¹⁄₂ pint/1¹⁄₄ cups full cream
   (whole) milk
1 egg, plus 1 egg yolk
finely grated rind of 1 orange
30ml/2 tbsp caster (superfine) sugar
vegetable oil, for frying

TO FINISH
250g/9oz/generous 1 cup mascarpone
15ml/1 tbsp icing (confectioners') sugar
90ml/6 tbsp single (light) cream
45ml/3 tbsp Cointreau or orange juice
500ml/17fl oz/2¹⁄₄ cups orange sorbet
icing sugar, for dusting

1 Blend the flour, milk, egg, egg yolk, orange rind and sugar in a food processor until smooth. Pour into a jug (pitcher) and leave for 30 minutes.

2 Heat a little oil in a medium frying pan or crêpe pan until very hot. Drain off the excess. Pour a little batter into the pan, tilting it so that the batter coats the base thinly. Pour any excess back into the jug.

3 Cook until the underside is golden, then flip and cook the other side. Slide on to a plate. Cook seven more,

lightly oiling the pan each time.

4 Preheat the oven to 200°C/400°F/Gas 6. In a bowl, beat the mascarpone, the icing sugar, cream and liqueur or orange juice until smooth. Spread the mixture on the crêpes, taking it almost to the edges.

5 Scoop and arrange shavings of sorbet to one side of each crêpe. Fold the crêpes in half and dust with icing sugar. Fold again into quarters and dust again.

6 Bake the crêpes in a shallow baking

Nutritional information per portion: Energy 316kcal/1324kJ; Protein 5.6g; Carbohydrate 34.2g, of which sugars 19.6g; Fat 17.2g, of which saturates 10.1g; Cholesterol 103mg; Calcium 100mg; Fibre 0.6g; Sodium 152mg.

Coffee pavlova with exotic fruits

Both Australia and New Zealand claim to have invented this fluffy meringue named after the ballerina Anna Pavlova. The secret of success is to leave the meringue in the oven until completely cooled, as a sudden change in temperature will make it crack.

SERVES 6–8

30ml/2 tbsp ground coffee, e.g. mocha
    orange-flavoured
30ml/2 tbsp near-boiling water
3 egg whites
2.5ml/½ tsp cream of tartar
175g/6oz/scant 1 cup caster (superfine)
    sugar
5ml/1 tsp cornflour (cornstarch), sifted

FOR THE FILLING
150ml/¼ pint/⅔ cup double (heavy) cream
5ml/1 tsp orange flower water
150ml/¼ pint/⅔ cup crème fraîche
500g/1¼lb sliced exotic fruits, such as
    mango, papaya and kiwi
15ml/1 tbsp icing (confectioner's) sugar

1 Preheat the oven to 140°C/275°F/Gas 1. Draw a 20cm/8in circle on non-stick baking parchment. Place pencil-side down on a baking sheet.

2 Put the coffee in a small bowl and pour the hot water over. Leave to infuse for 4 minutes, then strain through a very fine sieve.

3 Whisk the egg whites with the cream of tartar until stiff, but not dry. Gradually whisk in the sugar until the meringue is stiff and shiny, then quickly whisk in the cornflour and coffee.

4 Using a long knife or spatula, spread the meringue mixture on the baking sheet to cover the circle easily. Make a slight hollow in the middle. Bake in the oven for 1 hour, then turn off the heat and leave in the oven until cool.

5 Transfer the meringue to a plate, peeling off the lining. To make the filling, whip the cream with the orange flower water until soft peaks form. Fold in the crème fraîche. Spoon into the meringue. Arrange the fruits over the cream and dust with icing sugar.

Nutritional information per portion: Energy 296kcal/1238kJ; Protein 2g; Carbohydrate 33g, of which sugars 32g; Fat 18g, of which saturates 11g; Cholesterol 47mg; Calcium 37mg; Fibre 1.0g; Sodium 36mg.

Apple fritters with fruits

Fruit fritters make a delightful dessert – the aroma of the cooking draws you like a magnet. Serve them with a sweet sauce or compote or preserve of your choice.

SERVES 4

200g/7oz/1³⁄₄ cups self-raising (self-rising) flour
100ml/3¹⁄₂ fl oz/scant ¹⁄₂ cup full cream (whole) milk
5ml/1 tsp baking powder
40g/1¹⁄₂oz/3 tbsp caster (superfine) sugar
a pinch of salt
5ml/1 tsp butter
2 apples
vegetable oil, for deep-frying
icing (confectioners') sugar, to dust
Sweet sauce, to serve

1 Mix the flour and milk in a bowl and add the baking powder, sugar and salt. Melt the butter in a pan until it starts to brown, then mix it into the batter.

2 Heat the oil in a deep-fryer to 180°C/350°F. Peel and core the apples and cut them into thick rings. Dip them in the batter, making sure that they are completely covered, then drop them straight into the hot oil and deep-fry for 2–3 minutes, until the batter is crisp and golden brown.

3 Drain the fritters on kitchen paper, dust with icing sugar and serve immediately with the sauce.

VARIATION

To make your own sweet fruit compote, lightly poach a mixture of berries with sugar, rum and water.

Nutritional information per portion: Energy 391kcal/1644kJ; Protein 5.5g; Carbohydrate 54g, of which sugars 16.8g; Fat 18.6g, of which saturates 2.8g; Cholesterol 4mg; Calcium 213mg; Fibre 2.4g; Sodium 205mg

Summer pudding

This stunning dessert is an essential part of the English summer and it is deceptively simple to make. Use a mixture of fresh seasonal soft fruits and a good quality loaf of white bread.

SERVES 4–6

about 8 x 1cm/½ in-thick slices of day-
   old white bread, with crusts removed
800g/1¾ lb/6–7 cups mixed berries, such
   as strawberries, raspberries,
   blackcurrants, redcurrants
   and blueberries
50g/2oz/¼ cup golden caster
   (superfine) sugar
lightly whipped double (heavy) cream or
   thick yogurt, to serve (optional)

1 Trim a slice of bread to fit in the base of a 1.2 litre/2 pint/5 cup bowl, then trim another 5–6 slices to line the sides, making sure it comes above the rim.

2 Place all the fruit in a pan with the sugar. Do not add any water. Cook very gently for 4–5 minutes until the juices begin to run. Leave to cool.

3 Spoon most of the berries, and enough of their juices to moisten the fruit, into the bread-lined bowl. Reserve any remaining juice for serving. Fold over the excess bread, then cover the fruit with the remaining slices, trimming to fit. Place a plate that fits inside the bowl directly on top of the pudding. Weight it down with a 900g/2lb weight or a couple of full food cans. Chill for 8 hours.

4 Run a knife around the pudding and turn out on to a plate. Spoon over the reserved juices and fruit, and serve with cream or yogurt, if you like.

Nutritional information per portion: Energy 192kcal/815kJ; Protein 5.2g; Carbohydrate 43.1g, of which sugars 22.1g; Fat 1g, of which saturates 0g; Cholesterol 0mg; Calcium 82mg; Fibre 2.5g; Sodium 245mg.

Brandied apple charlotte

Loosely based on a traditional apple charlotte, this iced version combines brandy-steeped dried apple with a spicy ricotta cream to make an unusual and very tasty dessert.

SERVES 8–10

130g/4¹/₂oz/³/₄ cup dried apples
75ml/5 tbsp brandy
50g/2oz/¹/₄ cup unsalted butter
115g/4oz/¹/₂ cup light muscovado
    (brown) sugar
2.5ml/¹/₂ tsp mixed (apple pie) spice
60ml/4 tbsp water
75g/3oz/¹/₂ cup sultanas (golden raisins)

300g/11oz Madeira cake, cut into
    1cm/¹/₂in slices
250g/9oz/generous 1 cup ricotta cheese
30ml/2 tbsp lemon juice
150ml/¹/₄ pint/²/₃ cup double (heavy) or
    whipping cream
icing (confectioners') sugar and fresh mint
    sprigs, to decorate

1 Roughly chop the dried apples, then place them in a bowl. Pour over the brandy and set aside for about 1 hour until most of the brandy has been absorbed.

2 Melt the butter in a frying pan. Add the sugar and stir over a low heat for 1 minute. Add the mixed spice, water and soaked apples, with any remaining brandy. Cook gently for 5 minutes or until the apples are tender. Stir in the sultanas and leave to cool.

3 Use the Madeira cake slices to line the sides of a 20cm/8in square or 20cm/8in round springform or loose-based cake tin (pan). Place in the freezer while you make the filling.

4 Beat the ricotta in a bowl until it has softened, then stir in the apple mixture and lemon juice. Whip the cream in a separate bowl and fold it in. Spoon the mixture into the lined tin and level the surface. Cover and freeze overnight.

5 Transfer to the refridgerator 1 hour before serving. Invert it on to a serving plate, dust with icing sugar, and decorate with mint sprigs.

Nutritional information per portion: Energy 373kcal/1558kJ; Protein 5g; Carbohydrate 40.6g, of which sugars 34g; Fat 20.4g, of which saturates 12.4g; Cholesterol 42mg; Calcium 41mg; Fibre 1.2g; Sodium 152mg.

Lemon tart

This wonderfully tangy lemon tart uses lots of freshly grated lemon rind for a really intense flavour. Serve it cold with a small glass of Limoncello for a delicious grown-up dessert.

SERVES 6

250g/9oz/2¼ cups plain (all-purpose) flour, plus extra for dusting
125g/4¼oz/generous ½ cup cold unsalted butter, chopped, plus softened butter for greasing
115g/4oz/½ cup caster (superfine) sugar
1 egg, plus 1 egg yolk
icing (confectioners') sugar, for dusting

FOR THE FILLING

250ml/8fl oz/generous 1 cup custard
115g/4oz/½ cup sugar
finely grated rind of 3–4 lemons
250g/9oz/generous 1 cup ricotta cheese
1 egg, beaten

1 Put the plain flour in a bowl. Add the chopped butter and rub it in until the mixture resembles fine breadcrumbs.

2 Stir in the sugar and add the egg and egg yolk. Mix to a soft dough. Knead lightly, wrap in clear film (plastic wrap) and chill until required.

3 While the pastry is resting, make the filling. Heat the custard and stir in the sugar and lemon rind until the sugar is dissolved, then cover the surface of the custard with baking parchment and leave it to cool.

4 Preheat the oven to 180°C/350°F/Gas 4. Grease a 20cm/8in tart tin (pan) with butter. Beat the ricotta into the custard, then add the beaten egg. Mix thoroughly.

5 On a large sheet of baking parchment, roll out the pastry using a lightly floured rolling pin. Line the tart tin and trim the edges.

6 Pour the lemon filling into the tart case and bake in the oven for 30 minutes. Leave to cool, then dust with icing sugar. Serve at room temperature or cold.

Nutritional information per portion: Energy 605kcal/2539kJ; Protein 12.2g; Carbohydrate 80.5g, of which sugars 46.7g; Fat 28.3g, of which saturates 15.9g; Cholesterol 162mg; Calcium 149mg; Fibre 1.3g; Sodium 218mg.

Boston banoffee pie

This sumptuous combination of deliciously biscuity pastry, fudge-toffee filling and sliced banana topping will prove irresistible, and is wonderfully easy to make.

SERVES 6

115g/4oz/¹/₂ cup butter, diced
200g/7oz can skimmed, sweetened condensed milk
115g/4oz/¹/₂ cup soft brown sugar
30ml/2 tbsp golden (light corn) syrup
2 small bananas, sliced
a little lemon juice
whipped cream, to decorate
5ml/1 tsp grated plain (semisweet) chocolate

FOR THE PASTRY

150g/5oz/1¹/₄ cups plain (all-purpose) flour
115g/4oz/¹/₂ cup butter, diced
50g/2oz/¹/₄ cup caster (superfine) sugar

1 Preheat the oven to 160°C/325°F/ Gas 3. In a food processor, process the flour and diced butter until crumbed. Stir in the caster sugar and mix to form a soft, pliable dough.

2 Press into a 20cm/8in loose-based flan tin (pan). Bake for 30 minutes.

3 To make the filling, place the butter in a pan with the condensed milk, brown sugar and syrup. Heat gently, stirring, until the butter has melted and the sugar has dissolved.

4 Bring to a gentle boil and cook for 7–10 minutes, stirring constantly, until the mixture thickens and turns a light caramel colour.

5 Pour the hot caramel filling into the pastry case and leave until completely cold. Sprinkle the banana slices with lemon juice and arrange in overlapping circles on top of the filling, leaving a gap in the centre. Pipe a generous swirl of whipped cream in the centre and sprinkle with the grated chocolate.

Nutritional information per portion: Energy 608kcal/2547kJ; Protein 6.4g; Carbohydrate 78.5g, of which sugars 58.9g; Fat 32g, of which saturates 20.1g; Cholesterol 82mg; Calcium 246mg; Fibre 0.8g; Sodium 211mg.

Mississippi mud pie

Mud, mud, glorious mud – isn't that what the song says? Well, you can't get much more glorious than this – its status as a popular classic is definitely well-earned.

SERVES 6–8

250g/9oz/2¼ cups plain (all-purpose) flour
150g/5oz/²/₃ cup unsalted butter
2 egg yolks
15–30ml/1–2 tbsp iced water

FOR THE FILLING
3 eggs, separated
20ml/4 tsp cornflour (cornstarch)
75g/3oz/⅓ cup caster (superfine) sugar
400ml/14fl oz/1¾ cups full cream
   (whole) milk

150g/5oz plain (semisweet) chocolate,
   broken into squares
5ml/1 tsp vanilla extract
1 sachet powdered gelatine
45ml/3 tbsp water
30ml/2 tbsp dark rum

FOR THE TOPPING
175g/6fl oz/¾ cup double (heavy)
   cream, whipped
chocolate curls, to decorate

1 Sift the flour into a bowl and rub in the butter until the mixture resembles coarse breadcrumbs. Stir in the egg yolks with just enough iced water to bind the mixture to a soft dough. Roll out on a lightly floured surface and line a deep 23cm/9in flan tin (pan). Chill for 30 minutes.

2 Preheat the oven to 190°C/375°F/Gas 5. Prick the pastry with a fork, cover with baking parchment and baking beans and bake blind for 10 minutes. Remove the beans and paper, return to the oven and bake for 10 minutes more.

3 Mix the egg yolks, cornflour and 30ml/2 tbsp of the sugar in a bowl. Heat the milk and beat into the mixture. Return to a pan and stir over a low heat until the custard is smooth. Pour half the custard into a bowl. Melt the chocolate and stir into the custard with the vanilla extract. Spread in the pastry case, cover closely, then chill until set.

4 Sprinkle the gelatine over the water in a heatproof bowl, leave until spongy, then place over simmering water until the gelatine has dissolved. Stir into the remaining custard, with the rum. Whisk the egg whites until stiff peaks form, whisk in the remaining sugar, then fold into the custard before it sets. Spoon over the chocolate custard. Chill, then put the pie on a serving plate. Spread whipped cream over the top and sprinkle with chocolate curls.

Nutritional information per portion: Energy 571kcal/2385kJ; Protein 9.4g; Carbohydrate 53.5g, of which sugars 22.7g; Fat 36.2g, of which saturates 21.2g; Cholesterol 196mg; Calcium 160mg; Fibre 1.3g; Sodium 180mg.

Baked caramel custard

Custards are classic nursery puddings: this is a more sophisticated take on these simple, nourishing desserts. Known as crème caramel in France and flan in Spain, this chilled custard has a rich caramel flavour which is wonderful with cream and strawberries.

SERVES 6–8

250g/9oz/1¼ cups sugar
1 vanilla pod (bean) or 10ml/2 tsp vanilla
   extract
425ml/15fl oz/1¾ cups double (heavy)
   cream

5 large (US extra large) eggs, plus 2 extra
   yolks
thick cream and fresh strawberries, to serve

1 Put 175g/6oz/generous ¾ cup of the sugar in a small heavy pan with just enough water to moisten the sugar. Bring to the boil over a high heat, swirling the pan until the sugar is dissolved completely. Boil for about 5 minutes, without stirring, until the syrup turns a dark caramel colour.

2 Working quickly, pour the caramel into a 1 litre/1¾ pint/4 cup soufflé dish. Holding the dish with oven gloves, carefully swirl the dish to coat the base and sides evenly with the hot caramel mixture. Work quickly as the caramel soon sets and becomes hard. Set the dish aside to cool.

3 Preheat the oven to 160°C/325°F/Gas 3. With a small sharp knife, carefully split the vanilla pod lengthways and scrape the black seeds into a pan. Add the cream and bring just to the boil over a medium-high heat, stirring frequently. Remove the pan from the heat, cover and set aside for about 20 minutes to cool.

4 In a bowl, whisk the eggs and egg yolks with the remaining sugar for 2–3 minutes until smooth and creamy. Whisk in the hot cream and carefully strain the mixture into the caramel-lined dish. Cover tightly with foil. Place the dish in a roasting pan and pour in just enough boiling water to come halfway up the side of the dish.

5 Bake the custard for 40–45 minutes until just set. To test whether the custard is set, insert a knife about 5cm/2in from the edge; if it comes out clean, the custard should be ready. Remove the soufflé dish from the roasting pan and leave to cool for at least 30 minutes, then place in the refrigerator and chill overnight.

6 To turn out, carefully run a sharp knife around the edge of the dish to loosen the custard.

7 Cover the dish with a serving plate and, holding them together very tightly, invert the dish and plate, allowing the custard to drop down on to the plate. Gently lift one edge of the dish, allowing the caramel to run down over the sides and on to the plate, then carefully lift off the dish. Serve with thick cream and fresh strawberries.

VARIATION
For a special occasion, make individual baked custards in ramekin dishes. Coat 6–8 ramekins with the caramel and divide the custard mixture among them. Bake, in a roasting tin of water, for 25–30 minutes or until set. Slice the strawberries and marinate them in a little sugar and a dessert wine, such as Muscat.

Nutritional information per portion: Energy 622kcal/2587kJ; Protein 9.6g; Carbohydrate 44.8g, of which sugars 44.8g; Fat 46.4g, of which saturates 26g; Cholesterol 386mg; Calcium 98mg; Fibre 0g; Sodium 103mg.

Saffron and cardamon crème caramel

Some chilled creamy custards are deeply traditional; others have a modern twist, as here. This is served with the rich, buttery cookies, ghoriba. The cookies themselves are delicious with tea.

SERVES 4–6

600ml/1 pint/2¹/₂ cups full cream (whole) milk

115g/4oz/²/₃ cup sugar, plus 60ml/4 tbsp for
   caramel

a pinch of saffron threads

2.5ml/¹/₂ tsp cardamom seeds

15–30ml/1–2 tbsp rose water

4 eggs, lightly beaten

60ml/4 tbsp boiling water

FOR THE COOKIES

200g/7oz/scant 1 cup butter

130g/4¹/₂oz/generous 1 cup icing
   (confectioners') sugar, sifted

5–10ml/1–2 tsp orange flower water

250g/9oz/2¹/₄ cups plain (all-purpose) flour,
   sifted

a handful of blanched almonds

1 Preheat the oven to 180°C/350°F/Gas 4. Heat the milk, sugar, saffron and cardamom until the milk is about to boil. Set aside. Add the rose water, then gradually pour the mixture into the eggs, beating all the time. Set aside.

2 Heat the 60ml/4 tbsp sugar in a small pan until melted. Stir in the water, holding the pan at arm's length as the caramel will spit. Let it bubble before pouring it into the dishes. Swirl the dishes to coat the base and sides. Cool.

3 Pour the custard into the dishes and stand them in a roasting pan. Pour in cold water to two-thirds of the way up the dishes. Bake in the oven for about 1 hour, or until the custard has set. Cool, then chill.

4 Melt the butter and leave to cool until lukewarm. Stir in the icing sugar and orange flower water, then beat in the flour to form a smooth, stiff dough. Wrap in clear film (plastic wrap) and chill.

5 Preheat the oven to 180°C/350°F/Gas 4. Grease a baking sheet. Break off walnut-size pieces of dough and roll into balls. Place on the baking sheet and flatten. Press a nut into the centre of each. Bake for 20 minutes, or until golden. Allow to cool slightly; when firm, transfer to a wire rack. To serve, run a knife around the edges of the crème caramel dishes and invert on to plates. Serve with the butter cookies.

Nutritional information per portion: Energy 969kcal/4065kJ; Protein 17.8g; Carbohydrate 120g, of which sugars 72.3g; Fat 50g, of which saturates 29.3g; Cholesterol 306mg; Calcium 338mg; Fibre 1.9g; Sodium 443mg.

Poached pears with chocolate

Tender, succulent pears are combined with scoops of vanilla ice cream and then submerged in a delightfully rich chocolate sauce for this splendid dessert.

SERVES 4

4 firm dessert pears, peeled
250g/9oz/1¼ cups caster (superfine) sugar
600ml/1 pint/2½ cups water
500ml/17fl oz/2¼ cups vanilla ice cream

FOR THE CHOCOLATE SAUCE
250g/9oz good quality dark (bittersweet) chocolate (minimum 70 per cent cocoa solids)
40g/1½oz unsalted butter
5ml/1 tsp vanilla extract
75ml/5 tbsp double (heavy) cream

1 Cut the pears in half lengthways and remove the core. Place the sugar and water in a large pan and gently heat until the sugar has dissolved completely.

2 Add the pear halves to the pan, then simmer for about 20 minutes, or until the pears are tender but not falling apart. Lift out of the sugar syrup with a slotted spoon and leave to cool.

3 To make the chocolate sauce, break the chocolate into small pieces and put into a pan. Add the butter and 30ml/2 tbsp water. Heat gently over a low heat, without stirring, until the chocolate has melted. Remove from the heat.

4 Add the vanilla extract and cream, and mix gently to combine. Place a scoop of ice cream into each of four glasses. Add two cooled pear halves to each and pour over the hot chocolate sauce. Serve immediately.

Nutritional information per portion: Energy 1014kcal/4255kJ; Protein 8.8g; Carbohydrate 145.1g, of which sugars 143.2g; Fat 46.7g, of which saturates 29.6g; Cholesterol 81mg; Calcium 206mg; Fibre 4.9g; Sodium 152mg.

Chilled chocolate and espresso mousse

Heady, aromatic espresso coffee adds a distinctive flavour to this smooth, rich mousse. Serve it in stylish chocolate cups for a grown-up dessert on a special occasion.

SERVES 4

225g/8oz plain (semisweet) chocolate
45ml/3 tbsp brewed espresso
25g/1oz/2 tbsp unsalted butter
4 eggs, separated

FOR THE CHOCOLATE CUPS

225g/8oz plain (semisweet) chocolate

COOK'S TIPS

• *For extra indulgence, serve with scoops of mascarpone or clotted cream*
• *Sprinkle with some chopped fresh mint to create an attractive dessert for a dinner party finale.*
• *Leave out the espresso if serving for kids who may not like the coffee taste.*

1 For each chocolate cup, cut a double thickness 15cm/6in square of foil. Mould it around a small orange, leaving the edges and corners loose to make a cup shape. Remove the orange and press the bottom of the foil case gently on a surface to make a flat base. Repeat to make four foil cups.

2 Break the chocolate into pieces and place in a bowl set over a pan of simmering water. Stir occasionally until the chocolate has melted. Spoon the chocolate into the foil cups, spreading it up the sides with the back of a spoon to give a ragged edge. Chill for 30 minutes or until set. Gently peel away the foil.

3 To make the mousse, put the chocolate and espresso into a bowl set over a pan of simmering water and melt. Add the butter, a little at a time. Remove from the heat and stir in the egg yolks. Whisk the egg whites in a bowl until stiff, then fold into the chocolate mixture. Pour into a bowl and chill for at least 3 hours. To serve, scoop the mousse into the chocolate cups.

Nutritional information per portion: Energy 694kcal/2901kJ; Protein 11.9g; Carbohydrate 71.5g, of which sugars 70.5g; Fat 42.2g, of which saturates 23.7g; Cholesterol 210mg; Calcium 67mg; Fibre 2.8g; Sodium 115mg.

Chocolate, rum and raisin roulade

This rich dessert can be made and frozen well in advance. Use vanilla, chocolate or coffee ice cream if you prefer, though all versions will be just as enjoyably indulgent.

SERVES 6

115g/4oz plain (semisweet) chocolate, broken into pieces

4 eggs, separated

115g/4oz/generous ½ cup caster (superfine) sugar, plus extra for dusting

cocoa powder and icing (confectioners') sugar, for dusting

FOR THE FILLING

150ml/¼ pint/⅔ cup double (heavy) cream

15ml/1 tbsp icing (confectioners') sugar

30ml/2 tbsp rum

300ml/½ pint/1¼ cups rum and raisin ice cream

1 Make the roulade. Preheat the oven to 180°C/350°F/Gas 4. Grease a 33 x 23cm/13 x 9in Swiss roll tin (jelly roll pan) and line with non-stick baking parchment. Grease the parchment. Melt the chocolate in a heatproof bowl set over a pan of simmering water.

2 In a separate bowl, whisk the egg yolks with the caster sugar until thick and pale. Stir the melted chocolate into the yolk mixture. Whisk the egg whites in a grease-free bowl until stiff. Stir a quarter of the whites into the yolk mixture to lighten it, then fold in the remainder.

3 Pour the mixture into the prepared tin (pan) and spread it gently into the corners. Bake for about 20 minutes until the cake has risen and is just firm. Turn it out on to a sheet of baking parchment which has been placed on a baking sheet and generously dusted with caster sugar. Leave to cool, then peel away the lining paper.

4 Make the filling. Whip the cream with the icing sugar and rum until it forms soft peaks, then spread the mixture to within 1cm/½in of the edges of the sponge. Freeze for 1 hour.

5 Using a dessertspoon, scoop up long curls of the ice cream and lay an even layer over the cream.

6 Starting from a narrow end, roll up the sponge, using the paper to help. Slide the roulade off the paper-lined baking sheet and on to a long plate that is freezerproof. Cover and freeze overnight. Transfer to the refridgerator 30 minutes before serving, dusted with cocoa powder and icing sugar.

Nutritional information per portion: Energy 474kcal/1982kJ; Protein 8.3g; Carbohydrate 47.5g, of which sugars 46.1g; Fat 27.5g, of which saturates 16g; Cholesterol 203mg; Calcium 117mg; Fibre 0.5g; Sodium 99mg.

Hot Puddings

Look no further than here for warming, sweet comforters to end a meal in divine style. Alternatively, simply indulge in the sticky, chocolatey, baked, crumbly, warm creations at any time of day, as the fancy takes you. Here are dishes from the nursery menu – rice, chocolate and steamed puddings, jam roly poly and fruit crumble – along with festive and celebratory essentials such as mince pies, apple cake, and shoofly pie.

Eggy bread panettone

Thickly sliced stale white bread is usually used for eggy bread, but the slightly dry texture of panettone makes a great alternative. Serve with a selection of fresh summer fruits.

SERVES 4

2 large (US extra large) eggs

4 large panettone slices

50g/2oz/¼ cup butter or 30ml/2 tbsp sunflower oil

30ml/2 tbsp caster (superfine) sugar

1 Break the eggs into a bowl and beat with a fork, then pour them into a shallow dish. Dip the panettone slices in the beaten egg, turning them to coat evenly.

2 Heat the butter or oil in a large non-stick frying pan and add the panettone slices. (Do this in batches, depending on the size of the pan.)

3 Fry the panettone slices over a medium heat for 2–3 minutes on each side, until each one is golden brown.

4 Remove the panettone slices from the pan and drain on kitchen paper. Cut the slices in half diagonally and dust with the sugar. Serve immediately, with the fruit.

Nutritional information per portion: Energy 344kcal/1442kJ; Protein 8.4g; Carbohydrate 39.5g, of which sugars 17g; Fat 18.1g, of which saturates 7.5g; Cholesterol 151mg; Calcium 89mg; Fibre 0g; Sodium 256mg.

Waffles with spiced blueberry compote

This recipe requires a waffle iron. If you have to buy one it is unlikely that you will ever regret it, since waffles are so popular and are equally delicious with other stewed fruits or maple syrup.

MAKES 20

25g/1oz/2 tbsp unsalted butter, plus
   extra for greasing
350g/12oz/3 cups plain (all-purpose)
   flour
350ml/12fl oz/1½ cups water
475ml/16fl oz/2 cups double (heavy)
   cream

**FOR THE SPICED BLUEBERRY
COMPOTE**

200g/7oz blueberries, fresh or frozen
15ml/1 tbsp sugar
5ml/1 tsp balsamic vinegar
a pinch of ground cinnamon
a pinch of ground cloves

1 To make the compote, put the blueberries into a pan, add the sugar, vinegar, cinnamon and cloves and poach for 5 minutes until soft and liquid. Bring to the boil and cook for 4 minutes to reduce the liquid. Keep the compote warm, or cool and store in the refrigerator.

2 Melt the butter. Put the flour in a large bowl and gradually beat in the water to form a smooth mixture.

3 Add the melted butter. Whisk the cream until stiff then fold into the mixture.

4 Preheat a waffle iron. Add a little butter to grease the iron then place a dollop of waffle mixture in the iron. Cook the waffles until golden and keep warm as you cook the rest, greasing the iron each time. Serve hot with the spiced blueberry compote and cream.

Nutritional information per waffle: Energy 189kcal/787kJ; Protein 2.12g; Carbohydrate 14.52g, of which sugars 1.18g; Fat 14.03g, of which saturates 8.62g; Cholesterol 35mg; Calcium 41mg; Fibre 0,85g; Sodium 14mg.

Leche frita with black fruit sauce

The name of this dessert means "fried milk", but it is really fried custard. It has a melting, creamy centre and crunchy, golden coating – what more sublime finish to a meal could there be?

SERVES 6–8

550ml/18fl oz/2¹/₂ cups full cream
   (whole) milk
3 finely pared strips of lemon rind
¹/₂ cinnamon stick
90g/3¹/₂oz/¹/₂ cup caster (superfine) sugar,
   plus extra for sprinkling
60ml/4 tbsp cornflour (cornstarch)
30ml/2 tbsp plain (all-purpose) flour
3 large (US extra large) egg yolks
2 large (US extra large) eggs

90–120ml/6–8 tbsp stale breadcrumbs
   or dried crumbs
sunflower oil, for frying
ground cinnamon, for dusting

FOR THE SAUCE
450g/1lb blackberries or blackcurrants
90g/3¹/₂oz/¹/₂ cup sugar, plus extra
   for dusting

1 Put the milk, lemon rind, cinnamon stick and sugar in a pan and bring to the boil, stirring gently. Cover and leave to infuse for 20 minutes.

2 Put the cornflour and flour in a bowl and beat in the egg yolks with a wooden spoon. Add a little of the milk and beat to make a smooth batter.

3 Strain the remaining hot milk into the batter, then pour back into the pan. Cook over a low heat, stirring constantly. (The mixture won't curdle, but it will thicken unevenly if you let it.) Cook for a couple of minutes, until it thickens and separates from the side of the pan.

4 Beat the mixture hard with the spoon to ensure a really smooth consistency. Pour into an 18–20cm/7–8in, 1cm/¹/₂in-deep rectangular dish, and smooth the top. Cool, then chill until firm.

5 Make the fruit sauce. Cook the blackberries or blackcurrants with the sugar and a little water for about 10 minutes until soft.

6 Reserve 30–45ml/2–3 tbsp whole berries or currants, then put the rest in a food processor and blend to make a smooth purée. Return the purée and berries to the pan.

7 Cut the chilled custard into eight or twelve squares. Beat the eggs in a shallow dish and spread out the breadcrumbs on a plate. Lift half of the squares into the egg. Coat on both sides, then lift into the crumbs and cover all over. Repeat with the second batch of squares.

8 Pour about 1cm/$\frac{1}{2}$in oil into a deep frying pan and heat until very hot.

9 Lift two or three coated squares into the oil and fry for a couple of minutes, shaking or spooning the oil over the top, until golden. Reserve on kitchen paper, while frying the other batches.

10 To serve, arrange the custard squares on plates and sprinkle with sugar and cinnamon. Pour a circle of warm sauce round the squares, distributing the whole berries evenly.

COOK'S TIP
In Spain, milk is usually drunk at breakfast or used for cheese. In northern Spain, the milk has a wonderful quality and has been given special status as a dessert ingredient. Most popular of all the milk desserts are **leche frita**, **flan** *and* **filloas** *(thin pancakes).*

Nutritional information per portion: Energy 272kcal/1150kJ; Protein 7.7g; Carbohydrate 48.1g, of which sugars 27.1g; Fat 6.8g, of which saturates 2.7g; Cholesterol 146mg; Calcium 151mg; Fibre 2.2g; Sodium 169mg.

Apple cake with vanilla cream

This is a moist and flavourful apple cake made with ground almonds, cinnamon and sweet eating apples. It is a sublime apple cake to enjoy at any time of day – brunch, teatime, dessert, and for any type of large gathering. The vanilla cream is a perfect foil.

SERVES 6–8

115g/4^1/$_2$oz/^{1}/$_2$ cup plus 1 tbsp unsalted
   butter
7 eating apples
30ml/2 tbsp caster (superfine) sugar
10ml/2 tsp ground cinnamon
200g/7oz/1 cup sugar
2 egg yolks and 3 egg whites
100g/4oz/1 cup ground almonds
grated rind and juice of ^{1}/$_2$ lemon

FOR THE VANILLA CREAM
250ml/8fl oz/1 cup full cream (whole) milk
250ml/8fl oz/1 cup double (heavy) cream
15ml/1 tbsp sugar
1 vanilla pod (bean), split
4 egg yolks, beaten

1 Preheat the oven to 180°C/350°F/Gas 4. Butter a 20cm/8in flan tin (pan) using 15g/^{1}/$_2$oz/1 tbsp of the butter. Peel, core and thinly slice the apples and put the slices in a bowl. Add the caster sugar and cinnamon and mix them together. Put the mixture in the prepared tin.

2 Put the remaining butter and sugar in a bowl and whisk them together until they are light and fluffy. Beat in the egg yolks, then add the almonds and lemon rind and juice to the mixture.

3 Whisk the egg whites until stiff then fold into the mixture. Pour the mixture over the apples in the flan tin. Bake in the oven for about 40 minutes until golden brown and the apples are tender.

4 Meanwhile, make the vanilla cream. Put the milk, cream, sugar and vanilla pod in a pan and heat gently. Add a little of the warm milk mixture to the eggs then slowly add the egg mixture to the pan and continue to heat gently, stirring all the time, until the mixture thickens. Do not allow the mixture to boil or it will curdle.

5 Remove the vanilla pod and serve the vanilla cream warm or cold with the apple cake.

Nutritional information per portion: Energy 541kcal/2254kJ; Protein 7.6g; Carbohydrate 39.7g, of which sugars 39.3g; Fat 40.3g, of which saturates 20g; Cholesterol 227mg; Calcium 122mg; Fibre 2.1g; Sodium 135mg.

Rhubarb and raspberry crumble

A fruit crumble can be eaten at any time of day and does prefer lashings of cream. If you can, use first of the season rhubarb when it is bright pink and tender.

SERVES 4

675g/1¹/₂lb fresh forced rhubarb, cut into large chunks
a pinch of ground allspice
grated rind and juice of 1 lime
175g/6oz/scant 1 cup golden caster (superfine) sugar
225g/8oz fresh or frozen raspberries
custard or clotted cream, to serve

FOR THE CRUMBLE
115g/4oz/1 cup plain (all-purpose) flour
a pinch of salt
50g/2oz/¹/₂ cup ground almonds
115g/4oz/¹/₂ cup cold butter
115g/4oz/1 cup blanched almonds, chopped
50g/2oz/¹/₄ cup golden caster (superfine) sugar

1 Preheat the oven to 200°C/400°F/ Gas 6 and put a baking sheet inside. Cook the rhubarb in a pan with the allspice, lime rind and juice and sugar for 2 minutes until the rhubarb is tender but holds its shape.

2 Pour the rhubarb into a sieve (strainer), over a bowl to catch the juices. Cool, and reserve the juices.

3 Put the flour, salt, almonds and butter into a blender and process until it resembles fine breadcrumbs.

4 Transfer to a bowl and stir in the blanched almonds and sugar.

5 Spoon the rhubarb into a large ovenproof dish, and stir in the raspberries. Sprinkle the almond mixture over the surface, mounding it up a little towards the centre.

6 Put the dish on the baking sheet and bake for 35 minutes until crisp and golden. Serve hot, with custard or clotted cream and the warmed, reserved rhubarb juices.

Nutritional information per portion: Energy 812kcal/3403kJ; Protein 14.2g; Carbohydrate 88.1g, of which sugars 65.1g; Fat 47.4g, of which saturates 16.9g; Cholesterol 61mg; Calcium 345mg; Fibre 7.7g; Sodium 191mg.

Baked bananas with hazelnut sauce

Bananas are completely transformed when baked in the oven, and the ice cream and sweet hazelnut sauce make this an even more luxurious yet simple dessert.

SERVES 4

4 large bananas
15ml/1 tbsp lemon juice
vanilla ice cream, to serve

FOR THE SAUCE

25g/1oz/2 tbsp unsalted butter
50g/2oz/½ cup hazelnuts, toasted and
    roughly chopped
45ml/3 tbsp golden (light corn) syrup
30ml/2 tbsp lemon juice

1 Preheat the oven to 180°C/350°F/ Gas 4. Place the unpeeled bananas on a baking sheet and brush them with the lemon juice. Bake for about 20 minutes until the skins are turning black and the flesh gives a little when the bananas are gently squeezed.

2 To make the sauce, melt the butter in a small pan. Add the hazelnuts and cook gently for 1 minute.

3 Add the golden syrup and lemon juice and heat, stirring, for a further 1 minute. Set aside and keep warm.

4 Slit each banana open with a knife and open out the skins to reveal the tender flesh.

5 Transfer the bananas to serving plates and add scoops of ice cream. Pour the sauce over and serve.

Nutritional information per portion: Energy 382kcal/1598kJ; Protein 5.4g; Carbohydrate 49.4g, of which sugars 45.7g; Fat 18.6g, of which saturates 7.6g; Cholesterol 28mg; Calcium 88mg; Fibre 2.1g; Sodium 106mg.

Bakewell tart

Although the pastry base makes it a tart, this delectable recipe, infused with almonds and with an irresistible base layer of fruit jam, is traditionally called Bakewell pudding.

SERVES 4

225g/8oz puff pastry

30ml/2 tbsp raspberry or apricot jam

2 eggs, plus 2 egg yolks

115g/4oz/¹/₂ cup caster (superfine) sugar

115g/4oz/¹/₂ cup butter, melted

50g/2oz/²/₃ cup ground almonds

a few drops of almond extract

icing (confectioners') sugar, for dusting

1 Preheat the oven to 200°C/400°F/ Gas 6. Roll out the pastry on a lightly floured surface and use to line an 18cm/7in pie plate. Trim the edge.

2 Re-roll the pastry trimmings and cut out wide strips of pastry. Use these to decorate the edge of the pastry case by gently twisting them around the rim, joining the strips together as necessary. Prick the pastry case all over, then spread the jam over the base.

3 Whisk the eggs, egg yolks and sugar together in a bowl until the mixture is thick and pale.

4 Gently stir the melted butter, ground almonds and almond extract into the whisked egg mixture.

5 Pour the mixture into the pastry case and bake for 30 minutes, or until the filling is just set and is lightly browned. Dust with icing sugar before serving hot, warm or cold.

COOK'S TIP
Since this pastry case is not baked blind before being filled, place a baking sheet in the oven while it preheats, then place the tart on the hot sheet. This will ensure that the base of the pastry case cooks right through.

Nutritional information per portion: Energy 700kcal/2919kJ; Protein 10.8g; Carbohydrate 57.1g, of which sugars 36.7g; Fat 49.9g, of which saturates 17.1g; Cholesterol 257mg; Calcium 110mg; Fibre 0.9g; Sodium 394mg.

Caramel rice pudding with apricot compote

Lift the dark, crisp skin of home-cooked rice pudding to reveal a sea of creamy caramel rice. If you don't like the skin, simmer the pudding on top of the stove for about one hour instead of baking it.

SERVES 4

1 vanilla pod (bean), split
300ml/½ pint/1¼ cups full cream
   (whole) milk
300ml/½ pint/1¼ cups evaporated milk
50g/2oz/¼ cup short grain pudding rice

FOR THE CARAMEL
115g/4oz/½ cup sugar
90ml/6 tbsp water

FOR THE COMPOTE
75g/3oz/6 tbsp caster (superfine) sugar
225g/8oz/1 cup ready-to-eat dried
   apricots
50g/2oz/½ cup whole blanched almonds
a few drops bitter almond extract
   (optional)

1 Preheat the oven to 150°C/300°F/Gas 2. To make the caramel, put the sugar and half the water into a pan. Leave over a low heat, without stirring, until the sugar has dissolved. Increase the heat and gently boil until it is a caramel colour. Remove the pan from the heat, stand back and add the remaining water – it will hiss and splutter. Return to a low heat and stir to dissolve the hardened pieces of caramel. Remove from the heat and leave to cool for 2 minutes.

2 Put the vanilla pod, milk and evaporated milk into a pan and bring to the boil. Stir in the rice and cooled caramel, bring back to the boil, then pour into a shallow 900ml/1½ pint/3¾ cup ovenproof dish. Bake for 3 hours or until a brown skin forms on top and the rice beneath is soft.

3 Heat the caster sugar and 300ml/½ pint/1¼ cups water until the sugar has dissolved. Add the apricots, cover and simmer for 20 minutes until soft. Stir in the almonds and extract, if using. Leave to cool, then chill. Serve the rice pudding warm with the cooled compôte spooned on top.

Nutritional information per portion: Energy 313kcal/1321kJ; Protein 9.6g; Carbohydrate 54.3g, of which sugars 44.3g; Fat 7.6g, of which saturates 4.5g; Cholesterol 25mg; Calcium 312mg; Fibre 1.9g; Sodium 147mg.

Whisky-laced mince pies

Mincemeat gets the luxury treatment with the addition of glacé pineapple, cherries and whisky to make a marvellous filling for these traditional festive pies.

MAKES 12–15

225g/8oz/1 cup mincemeat
50g/2oz/¼ cup glacé (candied) pineapple
50g/2oz/¼ cup glacé (candied) cherries
30ml/2 tbsp whisky
1 egg, beaten, or a little milk
icing (confectioners') sugar, for dusting

FOR THE PASTRY

1 egg yolk
5ml/1 tsp grated orange rind
15ml/1 tbsp caster (superfine) sugar
225g/8oz/2 cups plain (all-purpose) flour
150g/5oz/²/₃ cup butter, diced

FOR THE WHISKY BUTTER

75g/3oz/6 tbsp butter, softened
175g/6oz/1¹/₂ cups icing
   (confectioners') sugar, sifted
30ml/2 tbsp whisky
5ml/1 tsp grated orange rind

1 To make the pastry, mix the egg yolk with the orange rind, caster sugar and 10ml/2 tsp chilled water in a bowl. Set aside. Sift the flour into a separate mixing bowl. Rub in the butter. Stir in the egg mixture and mix to a dough. Wrap in clear film (plastic wrap) and chill for 30 minutes.

2 Mix the mincemeat, pineapple and cherries. Spoon over the whisky and soak. Roll out three-quarters of the pastry. Stamp out fluted rounds to line 12–15 cupcake tins (pans). Roll out the remaining pastry and stamp out star shapes.

3 Preheat the oven to 200°C/400°F/Gas 6. Spoon a little filling into each pastry case and top with a star. Brush with a little beaten egg or milk and bake for 20–25 minutes until golden.

4 Place the butter, icing sugar, whisky and grated orange rind in a small bowl and beat with a wooden spoon until light and fluffy. To serve, lift off each pastry star, pipe a swirl of whisky butter on top of the filling, then replace the star. Dust the mince pies with a little icing sugar.

Nutritional information per pie: Energy 195kcal/818kJ; Protein 1.8g; Carbohydrate 26.3g, of which sugars 14.8g; Fat 9.5g, of which saturates 5.3g; Cholesterol 35mg; Calcium 36mg; Fibre 0.8g; Sodium 75mg.

Hot blackberry and apple soufflés

The deliciously tart flavours of blackberry and apple complement each other perfectly to make a light, mouth-watering and surprisingly low-fat, hot pudding.

SERVES 6

150g/5oz/³⁄₄ cup caster sugar,
  plus extra for dusting
350g/12oz/3 cups blackberries
1 large cooking apple, peeled and
  finely diced
grated rind and juice of 1 orange
3 egg whites
icing (confectioners') sugar, for dusting

COOK'S TIP

Running a table knife around the inside edge of the soufflé dishes before baking helps the soufflés to rise evenly without sticking to the rim of the dish.

1 Preheat the oven to 200°C/400°F/Gas 6. Generously grease six 150ml/ ¹⁄₄ pint/²⁄₃ cup individual soufflé dishes with butter and dust with caster sugar, shaking out the excess sugar. Put a baking sheet in the oven to heat.

2 Cook the blackberries, diced apple and orange rind and juice in a pan for 10 minutes or until the apple has pulped down. Press through a sieve (strainer) into a bowl. Stir in 50g/2oz/¹⁄₄ cup of the caster sugar. Set aside to cool.

3 Put a tablespoonful of the fruit purée into each prepared dish and smooth the surface. Set aside. Whisk the egg whites in a large grease-free bowl until they form stiff peaks. Very gradually whisk in the remaining caster sugar until glossy. Fold in the remaining fruit purée.

4 Spoon the mixture into the dishes. Level the tops with a palette knife or metal spatula, and run a table knife around the edge of each dish. Place on the hot baking sheet and bake for 10–15 minutes until the soufflés have risen and are lightly browned. Dust the tops with icing sugar and serve immediately.

Nutritional information per portion: Energy 123kcal/522kJ; Protein 2.1g; Carbohydrate 30.1g, of which sugars 30.1g; Fat 0.1g, of which saturates 0g; Cholesterol 0mg; Calcium 38mg; Fibre 2g; Sodium 33mg.

Sticky maple and pecan steamed pudding

A steamed pudding can be flavoured with anything – maple syrup and pecan nuts are wonderful, and look superb when turned out, as here. Serve with lots of your own home-made custard.

SERVES 6

60ml/4 tbsp pure maple syrup
30ml/2 tbsp fresh brown breadcrumbs
115g/4oz/1 cup shelled pecan nuts,
roughly chopped
115g/4oz/1/2 cup butter, softened
finely grated rind of 1 orange
115g/4oz/generous 1/2 cup golden caster
(superfine) sugar
2 eggs, beaten
175g/6oz/11/2 cups self-raising (self-
rising) flour, sifted
a pinch of salt
about 75ml/5 tbsp full cream (whole) milk
extra maple syrup and home-made
custard, to serve

1 Butter a 900ml/1½ pint/3¾ cup heatproof pudding bowl generously. Stir the maple syrup, breadcrumbs and pecans together and spoon into the bowl.

2 Cream the butter with the orange rind and sugar until light and fluffy. Gradually beat in the eggs, then fold in the flour and salt. Stir in enough milk to make a loose mixture that will drop off the spoon if lightly shaken.

3 Carefully spoon the mixture into the bowl on top of the syrup and nuts. Cover with pleated, buttered baking parchment, then with pleated foil (the pleats allow for expansion). Tie string under the lip of the bowl to hold the paper in place, then take it over the top to form a handle.

4 Place the bowl in a pan of simmering water, cover and steam for 2 hours, topping up with boiling water as necessary. Remove the string, foil and paper, then turn out the pudding and serve with extra maple syrup and custard.

Nutritional information per portion: Energy 523kcal/2187kJ; Protein 7.7g; Carbohydrate 55.6g, of which sugars 29.9g; Fat 31.6g, of which saturates 12.2g; Cholesterol 108mg; Calcium 160mg; Fibre 1.9g; Sodium 345mg.

Jam roly poly

This warming winter pudding, with its nursery-sounding name, first appeared on English tables in the 1800s. Boiling is the traditional cooking method, but baking produces a crisp golden crust.

SERVES 4–6

175g/6oz/1½ cups self-raising (self-rising) flour
a pinch of salt
75g/3oz shredded suet

finely grated rind of 1 small lemon
90ml/6 tbsp jam
custard, to serve (optional)

1 Preheat the oven to 180°C/350°F/Gas 4 and line a baking sheet with baking parchment. Sift the flour and salt into a bowl and stir in the suet and lemon rind. With a round-ended knife, stir in just enough cold water to enable you to gather the mixture into a ball of soft dough, finishing off with your fingers.

2 Remove the ball of dough from the bowl, and on a lightly floured work surface or board, knead it very lightly until smooth. Gently roll out the pastry into a rectangle that measures approximately 30 x 20cm/12 x 8in.

3 Using a palette knife or metal spatula, spread the jam evenly over the pastry, leaving the side edges and ends clear. Brush the edges of the pastry with a little water and, starting at one of the short ends, carefully roll up the pastry. Try to keep the roll fairly loose so that the jam is not squeezed out.

4 To bake the roly poly, place the roll, seam side down, on the prepared baking sheet. Put into the hot oven and cook for 30–40 minutes until risen, golden brown and cooked through. Leave the pudding to cool for a few minutes before cutting into thick slices to serve.

5 Alternatively, to boil the roly poly, shape the mixture into a roll and wrap loosely (to allow room for the pudding to rise) first in baking parchment and then in a large sheet of foil. Twist the ends of the paper and foil to seal them securely and tie a string handle from one end to the other. Lower the package into a wide pan of boiling water on the stove, cover and boil for about 1½ hours. Check the water level occasionally and top up with boiling water if necessary.

Nutritional information per portion: Energy 240kcal/1008kJ; Protein 2.8g; Carbohydrate 33.7g, of which sugars 10.7g; Fat 11.3g, of which saturates 5.7g; Cholesterol 0mg; Calcium 104mg; Fibre 0.9g; Sodium 111mg

Rich chocolate and coffee pudding

This is a delectable blend of coffee and chocolate with a surprising layer of creamy coffee sauce underneath. Add a generous helping of whipped cream for the perfect finish.

SERVES 6

75g/3oz/³⁄₄ cup plain (all-purpose) flour
10ml/2 tsp baking powder
a pinch of salt
50g/2oz/¹⁄₄ cup butter
25g/1oz plain (semisweet) chocolate, chopped into small pieces
115g/4oz/¹⁄₂ cup caster (superfine) sugar
75ml/3fl oz/5 tbsp full cream (whole) milk
1.5ml/¹⁄₄ tsp vanilla extract
whipped cream, to serve

FOR THE TOPPING

30ml/2 tbsp instant coffee powder
325ml/11fl oz/¹⁄₂ pint hot water
90g/3¹⁄₂oz/7 tbsp soft dark brown sugar
65g/2¹⁄₂oz/5 tbsp caster (superfine) sugar
30ml/2 tbsp unsweetened cocoa powder, plus extra for dusting

1 Preheat the oven to 180°C/350°F/ Gas 4. Grease a 23cm/9in square non-stick baking tin (pan). Sift the flour, baking powder and salt into a small bowl. Set aside.

2 Melt the butter, chocolate and caster sugar in a heatproof bowl over a pan of simmering water.

3 When the contents have melted, remove from the heat. Add the flour mixture and stir. Add the milk and vanilla extract. Mix with a wooden spoon, then pour into the baking tin.

4 Make the topping. Dissolve the coffee in the water in a bowl. Allow to cool. Mix the brown sugar, caster sugar and cocoa powder in a separate bowl. Sprinkle the mixture over the pudding mixture.

5 Pour the coffee over the surface. Bake for 40 minutes or until the pudding is risen and set. Dust with cocoa powder and serve with whipped cream.

Nutritional information per portion: Energy 325kcal/1371kJ; Protein 3g; Carbohydrate 60.6g, of which sugars 50.5g; Fat 9.5g, of which saturates 5.8g; Cholesterol 19mg; Calcium 66mg; Fibre 1.1g; Sodium 107mg.

Shoofly pie

An unsweetened pastry case made with a simple combination of butter and cream cheese complements the wonderful dark sweet filling of this pie from the American Deep South.

SERVES 8

115g/4oz/1 cup plain (all-purpose) flour
115g/4oz/generous 1/2 cup soft dark
  brown sugar
1.5ml/1/4 tsp each salt, ground ginger,
  cinnamon, mace and grated nutmeg
75g/3oz/6 tbsp cold butter, diced
2 eggs
185g/61/2 oz/1/2 cup black treacle (molasses)
120ml/4fl oz/1/2 cup boiling water
1.5ml/1/2 tsp bicarbonate of soda
  (baking soda)

FOR THE PASTRY

115g/4oz/1/2 cup cream cheese
115g/4oz/1/2 cup butter, diced
115g/4oz/1 cup plain (all-purpose) flour

1 Put the cream cheese and butter in a bowl. Sift over the flour, and rub in to bind. Wrap in clear film (plastic wrap). Chill for at least 30 minutes.

2 Preheat the oven to 190°C/375°F/ Gas 5. Mix the flour, brown sugar, salt, spices and butter in a bowl. Rub in until it resembles coarse breadcrumbs.

3 Roll out the pasty to a thickness of 3mm/1/8in and use to line a 23cm/ 9in pie plate. Trim and flute the edges.

4 Spoon one-third of the filling into the case. Whisk the eggs with the treacle. Put a baking sheet in the oven.

5 Pour the boiling water into a bowl and stir in the bicarbonate of soda; it will foam. Add to the egg mixture and whisk. Pour into the pastry case and sprinkle over the remaining filling.

6 Place on the hot baking sheet and bake for 35 minutes, or until browned. Serve hot or at room temperature.

Nutritional information per portion: Energy 472kcal/1975kJ; Protein 5.2g; Carbohydrate 53g, of which sugars 31g; Fat 28.1g, of which saturates 17.1g; Cholesterol 112mg; Calcium 201mg; Fibre 0.9g; Sodium 248mg.

Hazelnut pain au chocolat pudding

The ingredients of this pudding have been described as outrageous. This may be the case, but the dish is all the better for it. This decadent version of bread and butter pudding is equally at home as an informal indulgence and as a dinner party treat.

SERVES 6

4 large pains au chocolat
75g/3oz chocolate and hazelnut spread

FOR THE CUSTARD
300ml/¹/₂ pint/1¹/₄ cups full cream (whole) milk
300ml/¹/₂ pint/1¹/₄ cups double (heavy) cream

1 vanilla pod (bean), split
6 egg yolks
115g/4oz/generous ¹/₂ cup caster (superfine) sugar
icing (confectioners') sugar, for dusting
pouring cream, to serve

1 Butter a 1.7 litre/3 pint/7¹/₂ cup shallow baking dish. Cut the pains au chocolat into thick slices, then spread them with the chocolate and hazelnut spread. Arrange the slices, spread-side up and overlapping, in the prepared dish.

2 To make the custard, pour the milk and cream into a pan. Add the vanilla pod and place over a very low heat for 5 minutes until the mixture is almost boiling.

3 Meanwhile, in a large bowl, whisk together the egg yolks and caster sugar until light and creamy. Strain the flavoured milk on to the egg mixture, whisking well. Pour the egg mixture evenly over the pains au chocolat and allow to stand for 10 minutes to allow the pains au chocolat to absorb the liquid. Preheat the oven to 180°C/350°F/Gas 4.

4 Place the baking dish in a large roasting pan and pour in enough boiling water to come half-way up the sides of the dish. Bake the pudding for 45–50 minutes until the custard is softly set and the top is crisp and golden brown.

5 Remove from the oven and leave the pudding in the roasting pan of water until just warm. Sprinkle with the icing sugar and serve with cream.

Nutritional information per portion: Energy 1044kcal/4344kJ; Protein 15g; Carbohydrate 78g, of which sugars 56g; Fat 76g, of which saturates 41g; Cholesterol 416mg; Calcium 163mg; Fibre 2.5g; Sodium 709mg.

Sweet Asides

Confectionery treats are perfect for times when you want to spoil yourself. The sweet tastes and textures bring back memories of childhood tears lovingly soothed with a candy sweet. A luxurious drink, too, has the same pick-me-up role, whether a cool fruit smoothie or a chocolate float. The sweets and drinks here can be used either for special celebrations and gatherings or for private get-togethers.

Melting chocolate meringues

These little meringues are both chewy and crunchy, and filled with delectable flecks of chocolate. When they are baked perfectly, the meringue is slightly gooey and, if they are fresh from the oven, the chocolate is slightly melted.

MAKES 250G/9OZ

2 egg whites
115g/4oz/1 cup icing (confectioner's) sugar
0.75ml/⅛ tsp salt
2.5ml/½ tsp vanilla extract
100g/3¾oz dark (bittersweet) chocolate, chopped into pea-size chunks

1 Preheat the oven to 180°C/350°F/Gas 4. Line two baking sheets with baking parchment or silicone mats.

2 Combine the egg whites, icing sugar and salt in a stainless steel bowl. Place over a pan of just-simmering water. Whisk the ingredients to combine, then continue whisking until the whites reach 49°C/120°F.

3 Take the whites off the heat and transfer to a stand mixer or use a hand-held mixer with a whisk attachment. Add the vanilla extract and whip the whites until stiff and glossy peaks form. Fold in the chocolate.

4 Scoop the mixture into a piping (pastry) bag fitted with a large, round tip and pipe tablespoon-size blobs on to the baking sheets, about 2.5cm/1in apart. Pull away from the tops quickly so little points form.

5 Place into the oven and keep the door ajar with a wooden spoon. Cook for about 20 minutes, until you can move them along the paper easily. If they stick to the paper, they need 1–2 minutes more. Bake for less time if you want the inside more gooey.

6 Leave to cool completely. Serve immediately or store in an airtight container.

Nutritional information per total amount: Energy 1001kcal/4228kJ; Protein 11g; Carbohydrate 185g, of which sugars 179.7g; Fat 29.2g, of which saturates 16.9g; Cholesterol 9mg; Calcium 102mg; Fibre 0g; Sodium 438mg.

Coconut ice

The pink food colouring here is optional, but it looks lovely and similar to the iconic store-bought variety that is loved throughout the world. The use of coconut milk instead of milk in this version enhances the coconut taste. You could also add a splash of rum, which helps to cut the sweetness.

MAKES ABOUT 1.3KG/3LB

butter, for greasing
750g/1lb 13oz/3³/₄ cups caster (superfine) sugar
300ml/¹/₂ pint/1¹/₄ cups coconut milk
2.5ml/¹/₂ tsp salt
275g/10oz desiccated (dry unsweetened shredded) coconut
2–3 drops pink food colouring (optional), or any other colour you like

1 Grease a 20cm/8in square tin (pan) and line with baking parchment or waxed paper.

2 Combine the sugar, coconut milk and salt in a heavy pan and stir over a medium heat until the sugar has dissolved.

3 Bring the mixture to the boil, add the coconut and stir to combine.

4 Pour two-thirds of the mixture into the prepared tin, or all of it if not using colouring. Combine the remainder with a few drops of pink food colouring in the pan, then quickly pour over the first layer in the tin.

5 Smooth the top with an offset spatula, pressing down slightly.

6 Allow the coconut ice to cool. This may take a few hours.

7 Lift out of the tin by the sides of the parchment or waxed paper and place on a cutting surface. Cut into squares and serve. Store in an airtight container.

VARIATION
You can replace the coconut milk with an equal quantity of full-fat (whole) milk.

Nutritional information per total amount: Energy 4682kcal/19746kJ; Protein 20.1g; Carbohydrate 816.1g, of which sugars 816.1g; Fat 171.4g, of which saturates 147.4g; Cholesterol 0mg; Calcium 548mg; Fibre 37.7g; Sodium 452mg.

Honeycomb toffee

This recipe is a rich, traditional version of honeycomb toffee. To make it lighter in colour and taste, and to update the flavour, replace the black treacle or molasses with more golden syrup.

MAKES ABOUT 750G/ 1LB 13OZ

- 125g/4¼oz unsalted butter, plus extra for greasing
- 30ml/2 tbsp cider vinegar or white wine vinegar
- 100ml/3½fl oz/scant ½ cup black treacle (molasses)
- 200ml/7fl oz/scant 1 cup golden (light corn) syrup
- 400g/14oz/1¾ cups demerara (raw) sugar
- 2.5ml/½ tsp bicarbonate of soda (baking soda), sifted

1 Grease a 20cm/8in square cake tin (pan). Line it with a sheet of baking parchment so that each end of the paper comes up the sides of the tin. This will make it easier to remove the honeycomb.

2 Melt the butter gently in a large, heavy pan over a low heat. Add the vinegar, treacle, golden syrup and demerara sugar. Stir gently until the sugar has dissolved into the butter.

3 Turn the heat up to medium then, without stirring, heat the syrup until it reaches the hard-crack stage (154°C/310°F).

4 Remove the pan from the heat and immediately stir in the sifted bicarbonate of soda. As the mixture begins to froth, stir it once again. Take great care as the hot syrup bubbles up.

5 Pour the mixture into the prepared tin and leave it to cool.

6 When the mixture has started to set (after about 30 minutes), score the toffee with a knife into bitesize pieces.

7 Leave it to cool completely for a few hours before taking hold of the sides of the paper and lifting the block out of the tin. Break or cut into squares or rectangles. Store in an airtight container.

Nutritional information per total amount: Energy 3350kcal/ 14147kJ; Protein 4.4g; Carbohydrate 643.2g, of which sugars 643.2g; Fat 102.1g, of which saturates 67.5g; Cholesterol 288mg; Calcium 783mg; Fibre 0g; Sodium 1598mg.

Hazelnut praline

*Hazelnuts are the nut of choice in this delectable crunchy treat. Toast them to perfection –
if under-toasted, the oils will not be released and if over-toasted, they will impart a bitter taste.*

**MAKES ABOUT 600G/
1LB 6OZ**

200g/7oz/1¼ cups whole hazelnuts, with
  skins
butter, for greasing
60ml/4 tbsp water
400g/14oz/2 cups caster (superfine)
  sugar

1 Preheat the oven to 180°C/
350°F/Gas 4.

2 Spread the hazelnuts out on a
baking sheet in one layer. Place in
the oven. Set a timer for 7 minutes
and then check them. They should
have a golden colour and a good
firm texture. Cook them for a little
longer if necessary, checking them
often, until they reach this stage.

3 Empty the tray into a clean
dish towel and, while the nuts are
still warm, rub the skins off with
the towel.

4 Grease a sheet of baking
parchment with butter and place it
inside a baking tray. Transfer the
toasted, skinned nuts on to it so
they are in a single layer.

5 Now make the caramel. Combine
the water, sugar and cream of tartar
in a heavy pan. Place over a medium
heat and bring to the boil, stirring to
dissolve the sugar.

6 Once the sugar has dissolved stop
stirring. Boil the syrup until it
reaches the hard-crack stage
(154°C/310°F), then continue
cooking for 1 minute more.

7 Remove the pan from the heat
and immediately pour the syrup
over the toasted nuts.

8 Allow the caramel to cool
completely before breaking it into
bitesize pieces with your hands.
Serve immediately or store in an
airtight container.

Nutritional information per total amount: Energy
2876kcal/ 12094kJ; Protein 30.2g; Carbohydrate 430g,
of which sugars 426g; Fat 127g, of which saturates 9.4g;
Cholesterol 0mg; Calcium 492mg; Fibre 13g; Sodium 36mg.

Espresso-macadamia fudge

Macadamia nuts make the perfect partner for fudge, as their oily yet slightly crunchy texture complements the creamy texture of the fudge. The addition of coffee extract is merely to give it a little lift. Be sure to use the freshest nuts possible, as macadamia nuts have a short shelf-life.

MAKES ABOUT 1.3KG/3LB

750g/1lb 11oz /3³/4 cups caster
   (superfine) sugar
250ml/8fl oz/generous 1 cup golden
   (light corn) syrup
300ml/¹/2 pint/1¹/4 cups double (heavy)
   cream
375g/13oz milk chocolate, chopped
250g/9oz/1¹/2 cups macadamia nuts,
   chopped
75g/3oz/6 tbsp unsalted butter, cut into
   1cm/¹/2 in cubes, plus extra for greasing
5ml/1 tsp coffee extract or instant
   espresso powder dissolved in 10ml/
   2 tsp boiling water

1 Grease a 20 x 30cm/8 x 12in rectangular baking tin (pan) and line it with baking parchment or waxed paper.

2 Put the sugar, golden syrup and cream in a large, heavy pan and cook over a medium heat, stirring constantly, until the sugar dissolves. Then bring the mixture to the boil.

3 Without stirring, let the mixture cook at a slow rolling boil for about 10 minutes, or until it reaches the soft-ball stage (114°C/238°F).

4 Remove the pan from the heat and quickly stir in the chocolate, nuts, butter, and coffee extract or espresso mixture. Keep stirring until the chocolate and butter have melted and are thoroughly combined.

5 Pour the fudge mixture into the prepared baking tin and leave it to cool completely. This can take up to 8 hours.

6 Lift the fudge out of the tin by the sides of the parchment and place on a cutting surface.

7 Cut into squares and serve. Store in an airtight container.

Nutritional information per total amount: Energy 9614kcal/40330kJ; Protein 133.6g; Carbohydrate 1257.1g, of which sugars 1223.5g; Fat 501.6g, of which saturates 226.8g; Cholesterol 675mg; Calcium 1665mg; Fibre 22.3g; Sodium 1851mg.

Turkish delight

This fresh version of a sweet-shop classic tastes very different from many commercially produced versions, so it is worth trying even if you think you don't like it. The texture is soft and silky, and the aroma of perfumed roses with a hint of lemon makes these fragrant treats a real delight.

**MAKES ABOUT
1.6KG/3½LB**

butter, for greasing
450g/1lb/2¼ cups caster (superfine)
   sugar
900ml/1½ pints/3¾ cups water
2.5ml/½ tsp cream of tartar
75g/3oz/⅔ cup cornflour
   (cornstarch)
200g/7oz/1¾ cups icing
   (confectioners') sugar, plus extra
   for dusting
50g/2oz/¼ cup honey
rose water
lemon extract
pink food colouring

1 Grease an 18cm/7in square tin (pan). Put the sugar, 150ml/¼ pint/⅔ cup of the water and the cream of tartar into a pan. Stir to dissolve the sugar, then bring to the boil and heat until it reaches the soft-ball stage (114°C/238°F). Set aside.

2 Combine the cornflour, icing sugar and 50ml/2fl oz/¼ cup of the water in a heatproof bowl to make a paste.

3 Boil the remaining 700ml/1 pint 3½fl oz/scant 3 cups of the water and pour over the cornflour paste, whisking to combine. Return to the pan and simmer until it is clear and thick.

4 Gradually add the sugar syrup to the pan, whisking constantly. Boil for a further 30 minutes. The mixture should be a pale yellow colour and be rather transparent.

5 Add the honey and add rose water and lemon extract to taste. Add a few drops of pink food colouring.

6 Pour the mixture into the tin. Leave to cool completely.

7 Turn the Turkish delight out on to a board dusted with icing sugar.

8 Cut into cubes and toss in more icing sugar. You may need to repeat this if it absorbs a lot of the sugar.

9 Pack into boxes or containers with a generous amount of icing sugar to stop it sticking. Serve immediately or store in an airtight container for up to a week. Dust with more sugar if needed.

Nutritional information per total amount: Energy 2971kcal/ 12672kJ; Protein 3.9g; Carbohydrate 786.5g, of which sugars 717.5g; Fat 0.5g, of which saturates 0.1g; Cholesterol 0mg; Calcium 358mg; Fibre 0.1g; Sodium 84mg.

Dark chocolate truffles

Smooth, creamy and intensely chocolatey, these classic truffles are a decadent treat. Use the best-quality chocolate you can, as this is what will lend the truffles an extra-special edge. They are perfect for gifts, and look very attractive piled up in a box or tin or served in a glass bowl.

MAKES ABOUT 50

120ml/4fl oz/½ cup double (heavy)
  cream
100g/3¾oz/generous ¼ cup golden
  (light corn) syrup
1 vanilla pod (bean), split in half

350g/12oz dark (bittersweet) chocolate
  (66–70% cocoa solids), chopped
50g/2oz/4 tbsp unsalted butter, softened
unsweetened cocoa powder, for rolling

1 Stir the cream and golden syrup together in a heavy pan, then scrape the vanilla seeds out of the pod and add to the pan along with the pod.

2 Heat over a low heat and bring to just below the boil (a foamy layer of cream should just be starting to form). Remove from the heat, transfer to a heatproof bowl and cover with clear film (plastic wrap). Chill overnight.

3 Butter a 20cm/8in square baking tin (pan) and line with clear film (plastic wrap).

4 Place the chocolate in a medium stainless steel bowl and set over a barely simmering pan of water. Using a chocolate thermometer, heat to just below 46°C/115°F, then remove from the heat.

5 Meanwhile, place the bowl of cream golden syrup over a pan of simmering water and heat to just below 46°C/115°F.

6 Pour the melted chocolate and the cream into a blender and blend until it is thick and creamy. Alternatively, pour the liquids into a jug (pitcher) and blend with an immersion blender. Add the very soft butter, bit by bit, blending well between each addition so it is completely incorporated.

7 Pour the ganache into the prepared baking tin and smooth the surface with an offset spatula. Allow it to cool for a few hours and then chill until firm.

8 Turn the ganache block out on to a marble or other cold, hard surface. Remove the clear film. Dip a clean sharp knife in hot water, wipe it dry, then slice the ganache into 2cm/¾in squares.

9 Dust your palms and fingers with cocoa powder and roll the squares into rustic balls. Roll these in more cocoa powder. Serve immediately, or place the truffles in a bag or container with extra cocoa powder (to prevent them from sticking together) and store in the refrigerator. Remove from the refrigerator at least 30 minutes before serving, as chocolate should be eaten at room temperature.

VARIATION
Here the truffles are made into rough balls, but you could roll them into neater, more perfect shapes.

Nutritional information per truffle: Energy 62kcal/ 256kJ; Protein 0.4g; Carbohydrate 3.6g, of which sugars 3.6g; Fat 5g, of which saturates 3.1g; Cholesterol 9mg; Calcium 4mg; Fibre 0.1g; Sodium 6mg.

Chocolate brownie milkshake and ruby dreamer

For some lipsmacking indulgence, here are two divine ideas, one a fabulously tasty milkshake made with chocolate brownies, the other a smoothie using a pairing of ripe figs and ruby oranges.

**FOR THE MILKSHAKE
SERVES 1**

40g/1½oz chocolate brownies
200ml/7fl oz/scant 1 cup full cream
    (whole) milk
2 scoops vanilla ice cream
a little whipped cream
chocolate shavings or cocoa powder

**FOR THE RUBY DREAMER
SERVES 2**

6 large ripe figs
juice of 4 ruby oranges
15ml/1 tbsp dark muscovado (molasses)
    sugar
30–45ml/2–3 tbsp lemon juice
crushed ice

CHOCOLATE BROWNIE MILKSHAKE

1 Crumble the chocolate brownies into a blender or food processor and add the milk. Blend until the mixture is a pale chocolate colour.

2 Add the ice cream and blend until smooth. Pour into a tall glass and spoon over a little whipped cream. Sprinkle with chocolate shavings or cocoa powder.

RUBY DREAMER

1 Cut off the hard, woody tips from the stalks of the figs, then use a sharp knife to cut each fruit in half.

2 Pour the orange juice into a blender or food processor and add the figs, sugar and lemon juice. Process well until the mixture is really smooth and fairly thick, then pour into glasses and add crushed ice.

Nutritional information per portion (milkshake): Energy 637kcal/2652kJ; Protein 15.4g; Carbohydrate 54.4g, of which sugars 45.5g; Fat 41g, of which saturates 18.6g; Cholesterol 28mg; Calcium 416mg; Fibre 0g; Sodium 348mg.
Nutritional information per portion (dreamer): Energy 417kcal/1776kJ; Protein 7.2g; Carbohydrate 97.8g, of which sugars 97.8g; Fat 2.5g, of which saturates 0g; Cholesterol 0mg; Calcium 443mg; Fibre 13.8g; Sodium 96mg.

Honey and banana smoothie

The secret of the smoothie is always to serve it ice-cold. Whizzing them up with ice is the perfect way to ensure this. You can keep an ice tray of frozen orange juice at the ready – and it's a great way to add extra flavour.

SERVES 2 GENEROUSLY

450g/1lb/2 cups mashed ripe banana

200ml/7fl oz/scant 1 cup natural (plain) yogurt

30ml/2 tbsp mild honey

350ml/12fl oz/1¹/₂ cups orange juice ice cubes, crushed

FOR THE HOT CHOCOLATE SAUCE

175g/6oz plain (semisweet) chocolate with more than 60% cocoa solids

60ml/4 tbsp water

15ml/1 tbsp golden (light corn) syrup

15g/¹/₂oz/1 tbsp butter

1 First make the hot chocolate sauce. Break up the chocolate and put the pieces into a bowl placed over a pan of barely simmering water. Leave undisturbed for 10 minutes until the chocolate has completely melted, then add the water, syrup and butter and stir until smooth. Keep warm over the hot water while you make the smoothie.

2 Place all the smoothie ingredients in a blender or food processor and blend until smooth.

3 Pour the smoothie into big, tall glasses, then pour in some chocolate sauce from a height. This cools the thin stream of sauce slightly on the way down, so that it thickens on contact with the cold smoothie. The sauce swirls around the glass to give a marbled effect, which is very theatrical and sure to impress first thing in the morning.

Nutritional information per portion: Energy 901kcal/3790kJ; Protein 13.2g; Carbohydrate 148.1g, of which sugars 142.2g; Fat 32.5g, of which saturates 19.4g; Cholesterol 23mg; Calcium 253mg; Fibre 4.9g; Sodium 176mg.

Passionata milkshake

The combination of ripe passion fruit with sweet caramel is gorgeous in this dreamy milkshake. For convenience, you can easily make the caramel syrup and combine it with the fresh passion fruit juice in advance, so it's all ready for blending with the milk. For the best results make sure you use really ripe, crinkly passion fruit.

SERVES 4

90g/3½oz/½ cup caster (superfine) sugar
juice of 2 large oranges
juice of 1 lemon
6 ripe passion fruit, plus extra for garnish

550ml/18fl oz/2½ cups full cream
   (whole) milk
ice cubes

1 Put the sugar in a small, heavy pan with 200ml/ 7fl oz/scant 1 cup water. Heat gently, stirring with a wooden spoon until the sugar has dissolved.

2 Bring the mixture to the boil and cook, without stirring, for about 5 minutes until the syrup has turned to a deep golden caramel. Watch closely towards the end of the cooking time as caramel can burn very quickly. If this happens, you need to let the caramel cool, then throw it away and start again.

3 When the caramel has turned deep golden, immediately lower the base of the pan into cold water to prevent it from cooking any further.

4 Carefully add the orange and lemon juice, standing back slightly as the mixture will splutter. Return the pan to the heat and cook gently, stirring continuously, to make a smooth syrup. Transfer the syrup to a small heatproof bowl and set aside until it has cooled completely.

5 Halve the passion fruit and scoop the seeds into a blender or food processor. Add the caramel and milk and blend until smooth and frothy. Pour over ice and serve with a passion fruit garnish.

Nutritional information per portion: Energy 197kcal/828kJ; Protein 5.4g; Carbohydrate 33.2g, of which sugars 33.2g; Fat 5.5g, of which saturates 3.5g; Cholesterol 19mg; Calcium 179mg; Fibre 0.8g; Sodium 67mg.

Coffee frappé

This creamy, smooth creation for adults makes a wonderful alternative to a dessert on a hot summer's evening. Use cappuccino cups or small glasses for serving and provide your guests with straws and long-handled spoons.

SERVES 4

8 scoops of coffee ice cream
90ml/6 tbsp Kahlúa or Tia Maria liqueur
150ml/¼ pint/⅔ cup single (light)
   cream
1.5ml/¼ tsp ground cinnamon (optional)
crushed ice
ground cinnamon, for sprinkling

1 Put half the coffee ice cream in a food processor or blender.

2 Add the liqueur to the processor and then pour in the cream, with a little cinnamon, if you like, and blend. (For a non-alcoholic version, use strong black coffee, instead of a liqueur.)

3 Scoop the remaining ice cream into four glasses or cappucino cups.

4 Using a dessertspoon, spoon the coffee cream mixture over the ice cream in each glass, then top with a little crushed ice. Sprinkle the top of each frappé with a little ground cinnamon and serve immediately.

VARIATION
To make a non-alcoholic version, simply substitute strong black coffee for the liqueur.

Nutritional information per portion: 489kcal/2049kJ; Protein 8.3g; Carbohydrate 57.6g, of which sugars 55.6g; Fat 23.2g, of which saturates 15g; Cholesterol 73mg; Calcium 255mg; Fibre 0g; Sodium 136mg.

Cool chocolate float

Frothy, chocolatey milkshake and scoops of creamy chocolate and vanilla ice cream are combined here to make a meltingly delicious drink that will prove a big success with children and adults alike.

SERVES 2

115g/4oz plain (semisweet) chocolate, broken into pieces
250ml/8fl oz/1 cup full cream (whole) milk
15ml/1 tbsp caster (superfine) sugar
4 large scoops of Classic Vanilla Ice Cream (see page 152)
4 large scoops of dark chocolate ice cream
a little lightly whipped cream
grated chocolate or chocolate curls, to decorate

1 Put the chocolate in a pan and add the milk and sugar. Heat gently, stirring with a wooden spoon until the chocolate has melted and the mixture is smooth. Leave to cool.

2 Blend the cooled chocolate mixture with half of the ice cream in a blender or food processor.

3 Scoop the remaining ice cream alternately into two tall glasses: vanilla then chocolate. Using a dessertspoon, drizzle the chocolate milk over and around the ice cream in each glass.

4 Top with lightly whipped cream and sprinkle over a little grated chocolate or chocolate curls to decorate.

VARIATION
Try substituting banana, coconut or toffee ice cream for the chocolate and vanilla.

Nutritional information per portion: Energy 918kcal/3834kJ; Protein 16.9g; Carbohydrate 92.2g, of which sugars 91.5g; Fat 56g, of which saturates 33.7g; Cholesterol 11mg; Calcium 423mg; Fibre 1.5g; Sodium 208mg.

Cardamom hot chocolate

Hot chocolate is a wonderful treat at any time of day – for breakfast with a warm croissant, at teatime on a cold winter afternoon or before bed to help you sleep. Adding spicy cardamom gives this hot chocolate an extra rich, fragrant aroma.

SERVES 4

900ml/1½ pints/3¾ cups full cream
(whole) milk
2 cardamom pods, bruised
200g/7oz plain (semisweet) chocolate,
broken into pieces

1 Put the milk in a pan with the cardamom pods and bring to the boil. Add the chocolate and whisk over a medium heat until the chocolate is melted and the texture is smooth. The more you whisk the frothier the chocolate will be. Remove from the heat.

2 Using a slotted spoon, remove the cardamom pods and discard them. Pour the hot chocolate into heatproof glasses, mugs or cups and serve with whipped cream.

COOK'S TIP
Chop or cut the chocolate into small pieces with a sharp knife to enable it to melt quickly and evenly.

Nutritional information per portion: Energy 359kcal/1567kJ; Protein 10g; Carbohydrate 42g, of which sugars 42g; Fat 18g, of which saturates 11g; Cholesterol 6mg; Calcium 127mg; Fibre 0g; Sodium 100mg.

Creamy egg nog

Just the words egg nog suggest something rich and creamy. This drink has Scandinavian and American origins and is usually served cold, but this version is warmed up to bring out the flavour of the brandy and rum. So here is the egg nog in all its glory – with cinnamon sticks for stirring.

SERVES 4

475ml/16fl oz/2 cups double (heavy) cream
3 long strips orange rind
2.5ml/¹/₂ tsp freshly grated nutmeg
1 cinnamon stick
4 eggs, separated
30ml/2 tbsp caster (superfine) sugar
175ml/6fl oz/³/₄ cup golden rum
250ml/8fl oz/1 cup brandy
extra grated nutmeg and 4 cinnamon sticks, to serve

1 Pour the cream into a small pan, add the orange rind, nutmeg and the cinnamon stick and bring slowly to the boil. In a mixing bowl, beat the egg yolks with the sugar until really pale and creamy. When the cream is boiling, pour on to the egg mixture and whisk well.

2 Pour the mixture back into the pan and cook over a gentle heat, stirring, until it forms a custard as thick as pouring cream. Do not overheat.

3 Pour the rum and brandy into a pan and warm through. Stir into the egg custard. Whisk the egg whites until they form soft peaks and fold into the warm custard. Pour into a warmed punch bowl (or a heatproof glass bowl).

4 Sprinkle the surface of the egg nog with extra nutmeg to serve at the table or ladle straight into warmed glasses or mugs. Put a cinnamon stick (to use as a stirrer) into each mug or glass before filling.

Nutritional information per portion: Energy 928kcal/3832kJ; Protein 8.2g; Carbohydrate 9.9g, of which sugars 9.9g; Fat 69.3g, of which saturates 41.2g; Cholesterol 353mg; Calcium 91mg; Fibre 0g; Sodium 97mg.

Hot toddy

Also known as whiskey punch, this traditional cure for colds is more often drunk for pleasure as a nightcap, particularly to round off a day's winter sporting activities, and it is a great drink to hold and sip on cold, damp winter evenings.

SERVES 1

4–6 whole cloves
1 thick slice of lemon, halved
60ml/4 tbsp Irish whiskey
5–10ml/1–2 tsp demerara (raw)
sugar, to taste

1 Stick the cloves into the lemon slice, and put it into a large stemmed glass (or one with a handle) with the whiskey and the sugar.

2 Put a teaspoon in the glass, to prevent the hot water from cracking it, and then top it up with boiling water. Stir it well to dissolve the sugar and serve.

COOK'S TIP
All three types of Irish whiskey (single malt, pure pot stilled and a column-and-pot still blend of grain and malt) work well in this recipe.

Nutritional information per glass: Energy 149kcal/619kJ; Protein 0g; Carbohydrate 4.2g, of which sugars 4.2g; Fat 0g, of which saturates 0g; Cholesterol 0mg; Calcium 2mg; Fibre 0g; Sodium 0mg

Mulled wine

The enjoyment of mulled wine is strongly associated with Christmas, but because it creates a relaxing warm glow, it fits the bill for any winter's evening of merrymaking.

MAKES ABOUT 10 GLASSES

750ml/1¼ pints/3 cups red wine

**175g/6oz/scant 1 cup
    sugar, or to taste**

1 lemon

5cm/2in piece of cinnamon stick

lemon slices, to decorate (optional)

1 Put the red wine, 300ml/½ pint/1¼ cups water and the sugar into a large stainless steel pan.

2 Peel the lemon thinly with a vegetable peeler and add the peel to the pan with the cinnamon stick. Slowly heat this mixture over a low heat, stirring to dissolve the sugar, until almost boiling.

3 Remove from the heat, cover and leave for 10 minutes to infuse (steep). Strain into a heated jug (pitcher) and pour the hot mulled wine into warmed glasses, each garnished with a half-slice of lemon, if you like.

Nutritional information per glass: 120kcal/506kJ; Protein 0.2g; Carbohydrate 18.4g, of which sugars 18.4g; Fat 0g, of which saturates 0g; Cholesterol 0mg; Calcium 15mg; Fibre 0g; Sodium 6mg

Index